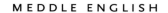

MEDDLE ENGLISH

CAROLINE BERGVALL
NEW AND SELECTED TEXTS

MEDDLE ENGLISH

NIGHTBOAT BOOKS CALLICOON (NY) 2011

ISBN 978-0-9822645-8-4

Design and typesetting by Kevin Mount
Text set in EideticNeo and Scala Sans

Cataloging-in-publication data is available
from the Library of Congress

Distributed by University Press of New England
One Court Street
Lebanon, NH 03766
www.upne.com

Nightboat Books
Callicoon, New York
www.nightboat.org

The front cover shows "the roundness of the earth explained" from
Gossuin of Metz, *Hier begynneth the book callid the myrrour of the
worlde*, printed by William Caxton in 1489. Reproduced by kind
permission, Glasgow University Library.

CONTENTS

heap of language
A heap of Language
A heap of Language
A heap of Language

I would like to make four points. Four short points about Middling English. The point about the midden. The point about the middling. The point about the middle. The point about the meddle. The midden, the middling, the middle, the meddle.

And a series of intersecting lines or tissues of lines. There are lines that draw from one node to another, one bell to the next, towards the architectonic structure, spatial resonant membranes of interconnections and tendencies. There are the obvious ones, the official line, the family line. The power lines, wired and electrical, electromagnetic landscapes, fibrous and spun. There are lines of travel, trade routes, blood routes. Intense seasonal species' traffic, migratory paths. Fields of uproots, departure knots, severance of the connects. Umbilical cords, lianas, plant ropes, hanging moss, epiphytes, headphones. Plumblines, sonars. Infralines of inseams, subvocalizations. The fine lines that crisscross between belonging, adhering, disappearing. Dissenting lines or lines of flight that sustain or dissolve under lines of fire, buzz lines, rumors. Songlines, memory structures, great pick-up lines. Outlines like edges, silhouettes, phasms, ghostings, x-rays. They set the wider configurations, the threadings that fall inunder a future perfect of English as language practice, what I call Middling English.

the midden

Let's imagine the midden of language. Robert Smithson brought a strong interest in geology to his views of language. Gordon Matta-Clark cut transversally through the structures of a condemned Paris apartment building. Let us cut a cross-section into building-stacks of language. What gets revealed is history and ground. Or rather, ground history, compost, history as compost. Temporariness and excavation. Volatility, weathering and renewal.

Principally, one discovers surprising varietals of soil, ancient yet compilable language bones, pressed word-fossils, collapsed layers, mineral toil, friable clays, dried pigments, decomposed fabric stretches, discontinuous tracings, and much unrecoverable matter. The top layers reveal a far larger extent of familiar elements, trace-able glossary, well-defined graphemes, syllabic conduits, what looks like mud-encased capitalizations, gold-dust, systems of numerical sticks, animal feathers, and various types of tools. These trace up letter elements historically, and through the altogether confusing and inventive arche-logics of etymology. Language is its own midden ground.

Letters, sounds, words are discarded from a language during accidental breaks. Or dispensed with, like outmoded cooking utensils.

Or pulled out, like teeth. Entire jawlines of these. Like the widely documented Runic and Old English voiceless fricative / Þ / thorn which after 1000 successful years as its own separate glyph disappears in the 14th century due in part to the absence of a corresponding letter-block in the new inscriptive techne of printing. More pronounced of course had been the drastic and planned simplification of syntax, and the removal of declension from English grammar. Nominative values hence less codified, relations between elements less certain, less explicitly coded. End letters and cases now thrown into the linguistic midden. Hierarchies to be confirmed and implemented differently, in more contextually regulated ways. Relations and irregularities tied to habitual assumptions and case work.

Writing records these fundamental ruptures, discontinuities, far more than it delivers stability. The blanketing of continuity appears as so many variations on silence and dominant rule. To locate characters with accent marks, non-English characters and additional symbols in our computer fonts today, still largely ruled by an Anglo-American control over digital linguistics, we have to go to the secondary block 128-255 of the relatively recent Unicode consortium, the first block being the basic ASCII.

The oral historian Alessandro Portelli, whose many interviews during the radicalized decades of Italy in the 1960-70s have made him a valuable thinker of the under-the-radar vitality of oral history for contemporary neo-liberalist culture, argues that fieldwork has to change the fieldworker, that it has to put them on the line, or there can be no useful knowledge acquired from the situation. This intimate challenge of the role of interviews in social science ensures a practice of local history that is firmly rooted in a wish to validate the impulses of the present, and transform the planned, recorded encounter into an uncertain transaction. For instance, about a song his research team has exhumed, he says: "The emphasis [from other critics] was on the fact that we were discovering these very ancient songs... It bothered me because what I had insisted on was not just that 'Donna Lombarda' originated perhaps in the eight century, but that it was being sung in the twentieth." It strikes me that this oral historian's prime interest in the singing of the song rather than in the exhumation of its ancientness is not that far removed from the way contemporary writers might relate to the explicit use of historic language detail: as a rich field of lived and deductive approximations, some based on ground research, some on the mysterious pleasure grain of the vocalizing, materializing text. A way of surfing the uneven, unruly canopy of present conditions without assimilating them to a dive in the past.

This work is not for the fake chime of heritage culture. Rather it exists for a proactive and politically "non-absorptive" purpose. The emphasis on liminal cultural excavation and grassroot activity addresses questions of language depth, of time retrieval through cultural proximity and singularized involvement. It does not for instance propose a buried and intrinsic connection between song and singer. This is certainly an interesting way of thinking, for the writer willing to break into the history of her language/s without becoming its prisoner. "We no longer reveal totality within ourselves by lightning flashes. We approach it through the accumulation of sediments" writes the Martiniquais writer and polemicist Edouard Glissant, who continues: "Sediment begins first with the country in which your drama takes shape." If this drama is also about the hold of identitarian politics and nationalism, he primarily seeks to go beyond this and imagines a translocal emphasis, what he famously calls relational poetics, based on a mixture of lived and acquired historical particularity and on an understanding of the confusing richness of history within language itself. One that looks for ways to integrate culturally, linguistically the voiding horror of the Middle Passage on Caribbean self-perception, by writing through and beyond the unspeakable:

The landscape of your world is the world's landscape. But its frontier is open.

The midden is method, and style. Intercepted notions of the past. The tracing up of re-emergents.

the middling

What is the middling of English? A middling is a smoothing over, a tense flattening, an artificial erosion, a surface stiffening. It is a blanket and a spread, a spread of green. Golf turfs are a good example of spatial middling. Heather Akroyd and Dan Harvey are two artists who only ever work with grass, turf, industrial nature, "living mini-lawn" as they call it, that "keeps its green color even under stress", and grows unimpeded into larger and larger structures. It happens whenever the mind of a language reorganizes blindspots into potholes, and diffuses or homogenizes political reality into sand-dunes, driving ranges, fairways and hazards. Lisa Roberston's *The Weather*: "Half and then half, delectable and idle, with gleams of fine greenery in the intervals. To the middle of instability, no absolution dad. To the end of surfaces, our mistake." Planned, inward-looking fertility, power: a fertilisation of the same. Explicitly having to unforeign one's name, to mask a regional or rural dialect. Passing to pass. Making language take a long soak in its own muddy bathtub. Virginia Woolf's unforgettable description of England at the beginning of the 19th century in *Orlando*. Middling in her book becomes a social and political region where dampness rules, values and feelings shrink, bodies are cold, sexes intensely separate and divided, their interactions minutely coded, language excessive and swollen by the damp's inescapable and pernicious influence. "Thus the British Empire came into existence."

Our weather today of course is thoroughly industrialized, globalization and environmental disasters are the measures of its seasonal currents, enforced migratory displacement mark the guarded bounds of turfed geographies. Political powers not so much flattened as flatlined. For the Jamaican poet Kamau Brathwaite, tidal poetics are the measure of a writing necessarily temporary, since compiling archives becomes physically impossible in the mudfloods, his own failing computer an analogical process of the devastation reaped by the hurricane season. The memory promise of writing here nullified, Brathwaite re-imagines the work of writing in a more performative and locative manner, through the "blinding" ideographic lay-out of his Sycorax environment. He wants readers to read more sensorially, recover another kind of memory structure. In actual fact, for a while, publishing these sycoraxed texts turns out to be surprisingly difficult as it stretches the complacent (not the technical) standards of much commercial or academic publishing.

A standard inevitably holds on to values that must stiffen articulacy and the rules of literacy in the name of a specific socio-political machine, and its historical legacy. This is reflected not only in impositions of pronunciation standards, and line formations, but also at macro level, in letters and their histories of use. In English, the letter H is the most durably complex that functions nearly like a shibboleth in the way it reflects class, literacy, political regionalism. The Irish playwright and socialist G. B. Shaw, who incidentally fought for and invested much effort and money in the creation of a new phonemic alphabet that would assist literacy enhancement for the many, saw in the always much frowned-on dropping of the H a mark of an irremediable social stratification and snobbism. There are those who take the opportunity of the visual glyph to remember the symbolic force of the trace itself. H becomes a fruitful bridge, a bilingual possibility and material connector at the start of Hélène Cixous's *Three Steps on the Ladder of Writing*. It is for bp Nichol the absolute passage between I and Self in his *22 letter alphabet*, "Aitch is I's magic ... one rotates into the other, palindromic." Regarding I, the French writer Monique Wittig found it necessary to split it right across the middle, "j/e". The reader would find themselves walking the shifter's plank of French pronominal use towards a queering of the entire language in her *Lesbian Body*. Let us play the I, le jeu du je, as a spatial break and passage from unspoken to speaking.

Some speech regulators and linguists contend today that British English is at threat of dissipation through its widespread top layer as a business-led lingua franca. This is an ironic development. Bolstering a standardized island language as prime export has long been part of a continued expansionist safeguard. The British Council's mission has, since its founding in 1934, always explicitly emphasized the international spread and training of the English language and culture. A controversial artist like Derek Jarman admitted that without its support his work might initially not have circulated as far afield as it did. On the dark side, its current *pep* project, Peacekeeping English Project, is meant to improve exchanges in English among international military and police personnel posted in areas of conflict. "English is the language of interoperability" announces its website, "for multinational forces to communicate effectively with each other."

The point is less whether it is a world language than the kind of world it perpetuates. The point is less whether it is a vehicular language than the kind of vehicle it charters.

Middling then an amnesic soak in landscaped language machine. Turfing the ground and the bounds of an exclusive and representative political language for as long as it will last. Maintaining that the French are not Francophones for instance. Or that the English are not Anglophones. The middling is protective levelling. Like making second-language learning optional in British schools or officially discouraging bilingualism in the home on the grounds that it affects integration to British society. One's integration or one's contribution? It is obstacle to influence, and rejects confluence. Like still finding gender, or race, as one's main outlook. A wipe out.

"Clearance of one organization to its opposite
is known as no man's
land..."
(Andrea Brady, *Wildfire*)

As the narrator Riddley Walker in the violent postapocalyptic novel of the same name has it: "What ben makes tracks for what wil be. Words in the air pirnt foot steps on the groun for us to put our feet in to."

The middling is a long embedded soak. Obstacle to flux and larger access. Language policies. Occupation, not occupancy.

the middle

At the end of the 14th century, the spelling and fixing of Middle English was very much up for grabs. Chaucer's decision to write in a spoken Southern English idiom helped to confirm the richness and versatility of a linguistic region that was starting to strongly de-frenchify its cultural language, de-latinate its vocabulary's antecedents, and revalue its Anglo-Saxon glossary, while Scandinavian roots were still especially clear and exposed in the syntax and glossary of the North. He made his choices from within the language's active maelstrom of influences and confluences. Everything about Middle English was a mashup on the rise.

The dispersed, intensely regional transformations of English active in the Middle English of Chaucer's days are again to be found in the inventive and adaptive, dispersed, diversely anglo-mixed, anglophonic, anglo-foamic languages practiced around the world today, as they follow or emerge from the grooves of military, commercial, cultural transport and trafficking. This transport flows across both diachronic and synchronic routes, sheds as much as it drags historical account along with itself. The wide reach and deep infiltration of Latin had eventually given way to the emergence of distinct latinate languages. English will eventually break and evolve into separate languages. The geopolitical and complex trans-English realities of many post-colonial nations are already exerting lasting pressure. Languages travel as seeded forms of themselves.

Spelling is ideal as a visual marker of such slow changes. It can shift a letter or word from being a semiotic sign to a semiological icon. It can confront the transformed territorialities of English itself. Radical forms of English spelling have dynamized, signed and performed the activist messages of many spoken/written acted up identitarian and revolutionary arts. Explicitly and efficiently spelling can act as a shorthand for cultural outmodedness and revolutionary revival. The K in Amerika continues to hit a raw institutionalized nerve. It is as iconic a sign as the red, green and black British flag created by artist Chris Ofili in response to Paul Gilroy's "There's no black in the Union Jack." Incidentally, its increased usage in preference to the /c/, also recalls the letter /k/'s preponderance in the Old English of pre-Norman times.

Today, a language's physical manifestation often extends towards electricity and surges. Mediated states, telematic socialization. Spelling daily actively tampered with and coded by shorthand wireless, enhanced by bicultural usage, consumer speed, and digitized mixed writing systems. A text takes on forms that extend language into electronics, data systems, aural proximities, means of generation and dissemination that affect the material and temporal traffic of a nodal series of "pages". The reader's body and skills have been diversifying accordingly: thumbs grow more flexible, ears are longer and prosthetic, eyes readily need the stimulus of a moveable text to read.

Writing of course precedes print culture and will continue after it. Being in formation, new media and communication technologies can help to identify the complex hold-ups to the renewal of the role of writing in culture. For instance, they signal that the forms of exchange and learning most widely sought today place transformative and connective value on locationality, transport and audio-visuality. So what will a contemporary writing environment require and for what purpose? And what is its role? How does it record and store itself? What are its essential elements and tools? How does it perform and how does it read? What does reading mean? How will memory function, what will transcription entail?

Increasingly, writing draws from literary as much as cross-media activities. It is signed through by literal as well as lettered bodies. Poetic art becomes an occupancy of language made manifest through various platforms, a range of instrumental tools and skills and relativized forms of inscription. From audio performance to complex events, it functions in a logic of relays and of distributive networks, incidentally already inherent in the permutational logic of the alphabetic and indexical systems. This is allowing a reinvestment of literary productions away from often stultifying distribution markets towards dynamic networks, systems of exchange and more open archival structures. If this seems on a par with the displacement of literature as a dominant artform, and publishing's hold on that, the diversification of writing culture goes also way beyond strategic survival or a timely fascination with media flexibility.

Indeed, beyond literary culture, all these questions and issues affect the cultural syntax itself. They are a reminder of the needs awaiting future literacy issues, both linguistic literacy (what we now call communication, multimodular training as well as speech production) and, not one without the other, cultural literacy.

The middle is slang. Processing of new literacy tools. Networks and distributive modes of knowledge. Writing in culture.

the meddle

Spoken, transmitted, inscribed languages are at the root of the imagination of writing. They highlight the social machines that underpin the work: the voices, the languages, the pleasures, the complex nexus of cultural and literary motivations with their access markers, their specific narratives, existential tropes, their polemical procedures and formal devices. It is the writer's role to test out, provoke the naturalized edges and bounds of language use and rules. She mines language for what is always moving, always escaping. To travel at the heels of writing activates reclaiming zones, fictitious collective memory.

So much holds our bodies, our lives, to separate identitarian account. How does one shift the representational stick-up from the face of the speaker?

I repeat what many have said, that poetic or art language must not implicitly be held to account of identities and national language, the seductions of literary history, or the frequently fetishistic methodologies of art movements, but rather seek, far and close, the indicators and practices of language in flux, of thought in making: pleasured language, pressured language, language in heated use, harangued language, forms of language revolutionized by action, polemical language structures that propose an intense deliberate reappraisal of the given world and its given forms.

More often than not, we each use a voice that speaks for us before we get to speak. Quite apart from the ideological implications and beyond palliative arts methodologies, this is why so many of us spend so much of our lives and imagination working at the undoing of a voice or identity we do not wish to be tagged as and questioning the methods of environments we might not wish to represent. It is through this confusing, seemingly self-defeating process of dissoci-ation, of "disloyalty", that other forms of allegiances are made manifest and other conductor channels can be generated.

To meddle with English is to be in the flux that abounds, the large surf of one's clouded contemporaneity. It is a process of social and mental excavation explored to a point of extremity. One that reaches for the irritated, excitable uncertainties of our embodied spoken lives by working with, taking apart, seeing through the imposed complicities of linguistic networks and cultural scaffolds. One which is not only prompted to recognizes what it wishes to fight against: what sedates, what isolates, what immobilizes, what deadens, what perpetuates. But works at it tactically, opportunistically, utilising at will and with relish the many methods, tools, abilities and experiential attitudes it needs. Making a workshop of the surrounding world. Oiling creativity and artistry with critical spirit, since there can be no revolt nor renewal without creative impulse, without anarchic pleasure, without a leap in the dark.

It means implicating one's own life through the gestures and events of one's work. Taking the risk of spitting it out, and of being spat out. There is only so much one should want to do to pass, to be passable, to appear to belong to today.

Anonymity — &onymity — of the writer whose masks have fallen deeply into the pits and currents of l&guage. Rebirth of the songer. Intense magnetism of lines that go through the body like radial songs.

My personal sense of linguistic belonging was not created by showing for the best English I can speak or write, but the most flexible one. To make and irritate English at its epiderm, and at my own.

Something crosses over comes. The borders are as long as the journey, etched in. Words disappear from all sides of the borders. A sudden surge of sweat on crossing the border. National, regional, urban borders, unknown streets, spaces, places, bodies, names, faces. Crossing into something, or someone. The borderline eats up the overspill, makes a long line of corpses. Dialogue is conflict, said the German playwright Heiner Müller. The apprenticeship of dialogue as encounter is necessarily a meddling of boundary, a heightening of points of internalized resistance or ideological differences. One's comprehension meddled with. Then, let us imagine it as contact, a point of uncovery. Rather than retaliation, a point of sharpened attention. Transitive directionality, transitive awareness.

The meddle is collective awareness. Denaturalization of one's personal and cultural premise. Getting lost. Physical and mental effort. New apprenticeship and transformed commitment.

SHORTER CHAUCER TALES

The fruyt of every tale is for to seye;
They ete, and drynke, and daunce, and synge, and pleye.
　　They soupen and they speke,
　　And drynken evere strong ale atte beste.
"Now lat us sitte and drynke, and make us merie,
　　　　And lat us dyne as soone as that ye may;
Lat us heere a messe, and go we dyn
　　　　The service doon, they soupen al by day;
And to the dyner faste they spedde,
　　and go we dyn
With hym to dyne
　　　　To come to dyner
And thus I lete hem ete and drynke and pleye,
　　　　But thus I lete in lust and jolitee
I lete hem, til men to the soper dresse.
　　They ete and drynke, and whan this hadde an ende,
Of mete and drynke,
　　　　And eten also and drynken over hir myght,
　　　　To eten of the smale peres grene.

They drynke, and speke, and rome a while and pleye,

    Ordeyened hath this feeste of which I tolde

Go

to feste

    at a kynges feeste

Each man woot wel that at a kynges feeste

    Hath plentee, to the mooste and to the leeste

Arrayed for this feste in every wise

    Whan he of wyn was repleet at his feeste,

They fette hym first the sweete wyn,

    And sende hym drynke,

And there he swoor on ale and breed,

    With bread and chesse, and a good ale in a jubbe

Cheweth greyn and lycorys

    With whete and malt

Both mele and corn

    be it whete or otes,

For male and breed, and rosted hem a goos

    That they han eten with thy stubbel goos

And beggeth mele and chese, or elles corn.

    Instide of flour yet wol I yeve hem bren

Than maystow chese

    Yif us a busshel whete, malt, or reye,

A goddes kechyl, or a trype of chese,

    Bacon or beef,

Seynd bacoun, and somtyme an ey or tweye,

    The bacon was nat fet for hem,

And of youre softe breed nat but a shyvere,
And after that a rosted pigges heed
    Milk and broun breed,
many a muscle and many an oystre,
    A cake of half a busshel fynde
many a pastee
        And eek the wyn,
The spices and the wyn is come anoon,
        Of spicerie, of leef, and bark, and roote
Ther spryngen herbes, grete and smale,
The lycorys and cetewale,
    And many a clowe-gylofre,
And notemuge to putte in ale,
Wheither it be moyste or stale,
    And roial spicerye,
    And gyngebreed
And lycorys, and eek comyn,
    So that men myghte dyne.
Bacus the wyn shynketh al aboute,
    And broghte of myghty ale a large quart
    And whan that each of hem had dronke his part
Now kepe yow fro the white and fro the rede,
    Whan man so drynketh of the white and rede
fro the white wyn of Lepe,
This wyn of Spaigne crepeth subtilly
    And thanne he taketh a sop in fyn clarree,
He drynketh ypocras, clarree, and vernage

Of spices hoote

Or else a draught of fresh-drawn, malty ale,

I hadde levere than a barel ale

Drynketh a draughte

drinken of this welle a draughte

Fecche me drynke,

He drank

And drank, and yaf his felawe drynke also,

Men drynken,

This messager drank sadly ale and wyn,

Nay thou shalt drynken of another tonne

Shall savoure wors than ale

For she drank wyn

She drank,

How fairer been thy brestes than is wyn!

Whan I had dronke a draughte of sweete wyn.

As evere moote I drynken wyn or ale,

But first I make a protestacioun

That I am dronke,

That for dronken was al pale

saugh that he was dronke of ale,

Ful pale he was for dronken

O Januarie, dronken in plesaunce

I wol drynke licour of the vyne,

I am wont to preche, for to wynne.

So dronke he was,

O dronke man,

Ye fare as folk that dronken were of ale.

And for despit he drank ful muchel moore,

      Lo, how that dronken Looth, unkyndely

For dronkenesse is

      And dronkenesse is eek a foul record

A lecherous thyng is wyn

A likerous mouth moste han a likerous tayl.

      Hath wyn bireved me myn eyen sight?

Ye shul have digestyves

Of wormes, er y take youre laxatyves

Of lawriol, centaure, and fumetere

Of herbe yve, growing in oure yeerd, ther mery is

Pekke hem up right as they grow, and ete heme yn!

      Til wel ny the day bigan to sprynge.

Here is ended the Host Tale.

THE SUMMER TALE (DEUS HIC, 1)

Rome is the hem home of ice cream
and for generations, burgeys and pilgrims ylyk,
this glade folk, in joye and blisse at mete,
have forsaken dessert at the Inn
for the simple plesance
of sitting outside with a takeaway cone.
The last Papa Pope Johannes Paulus Tweye,
a preest holy and gay,
used to have tubs of his favourite flavour, marron glacé,
delivered to his summer residence.
Thanked be God, in wele and habundaunce!

But if his successor, Pope Benedict XVI,
wants to see how Polish ice cream compares
during a viage trip there this wyke week,
Get us som mete and drynke, and make us cheere!
he is likely to be apayed a bit disappointed.
"For many a pastee hastow,
cakes and ice cream can easily go off

in summer temperatures and can pose
a danger to health, that hath been twies hoot
and twies coold",
a spokeswyf woman for local health bailiffs
quod to Agence France Press.
"That's why we're banning takeaway sales
on the day many pilgrim pilgrims
will be arriving in Wadowice".

And that isn't all that has made it
onto the liste of voided banned items.
Areas that the Pope will visiter,
including the citees of Warsaw and Krakow,
will be dry, with a ban on all licour sales while the Papa is in toun:
For goddes love, drynk moore attemprely!
Polish Mennes of Lawe seyen the ban is in place
to maintain public order and as a mark of respect for the pontiff.
No drynke which that myghte dronke make,
but there in abstinence preye and wake.

Papa Benedict XVI himself
will be offered both red and white wyn.
"Deus hic!" quod he, God is here,
as he attends houses of office stuffed with plentee,
a series of solempne gala sopers,
according to local media voys reports.
Television advertisements for licour

have eek also been banned.

Along with those for contraceptives, lingerie and tampons.

Chaast was man in paradys, certeyn.

"There is alwayes the risk that the faithful may feel hurt

how many maladyes,

folwen of excesse and of goltonyes!

if programming devoted to the Pope's visit

wedded to poverte and continence,

to charite, humblesse, and abstinence,

is interrupted by frivolous ads.

The body is so redy and penyble",

the heed of advertising for Telewizja Polska,

the state-run TV network,

told the Associated Press news agency.

BBC NEWS 25 May 2006.

Here endeth the Summer Tale.

THE FRANKER TALE (DEUS HIC, 2)

Following tweye two breathing crises
and with a tube placidly placed placed
in his esophagus, the papal Pope in Rome
global preacher most powerful suprem
o was not in good form
when the seeds of death's deeth
one by one finally popped in hym him
irreparably tearing the throat and the skin's hem.

Back at the Tavern in London
the dear vinolent drunken queer
painter portreytour
knew all along once ones
the hol hole of the hooly blessed
Sire Father's muth mouth turns
from screm to scream to smear
rising seated darkly in a white frame
of derk purple shoulders drenched in a shower of gold paint
it would be tyme, it's time

to deepen the denn, to coarsen the crust
and seek out the companye!

A new ideology of yvele evell evyl evil manaces society
and it includes gay weddynge jolly marriage
abortion abomination and stem cell studie research
wrote the papal he hey in his bestselling scriptures book,
Memory and Identity.
The Pope's noisy mouth had a mutt
and a deceptively brooding chin.
Ones once both saufly safely shut ad eternam
papal knights guards were quickly positioned.
There will be no collective revelrye,
gaiety merrymaking, drynke drinking,
daunce dancing on tabules tables
or shaking one's booty aboute around
or laying the shrewed cursed poisoned
yifte gift of one's maladye
this sickness our need at the feet of the lifeless pontiff.
A sea of pilgrims mourn move in sylent silent procession
past the hooly holy cors corpse careyne carcass arrayed laid-out
prepared solempnely in full ceremony.
But this deethly Death is short-lived.
Soon cries rise from Seint Peter's square:
The Pope is dead! Long live the Pope's Rottweiler!

'*Beloved Sisters in the Lord!*'
(Letter to Women, 10 July 1995
on the occasion of the Fourth World Conference on Women, Beijing)
To grope tendrely a conscience
In shrift; in prechyng is my diligence,
I walk and I walke, I fish and I fisshe
his word is set al myn entente to spread intent.
'*I greet you all most cordially, women throughout the world!*
What great appreciation must be shown to those women who, with
a heroic love for the child they have conceived, proceed with a
pregnancy resulting from the injustice of rape. Here we are thinking
of atrocities perpetrated not only in situations of war, still so
common in the world, but also in societies which are blessed by
prosperity and peace and yet are often corrupted by a culture of
hedonistic permissiveness. The choice to have an abortion always
remains a grave sin.'

The wholly painter staring blankly stands between two animal carcasses
suspended on hooks has his photograph taken.
Women of Bosnia! Women of Rwanda! Women of Afghanistan!
Women of Bengal! Kurdish women! Women of Chechnya!
Whan thirty tyrants, ful of cursednesse,
Hadde slayn Phidoun in Atthenes, at feste,
They comanded his daughters for tareste,
And bryngen hem biforn hem in despit,
Al naked, to fulfille hir foul delit, their foul delight
And in hir fadres blood their father's blood they made them dance

Upon the pavement, God yeve hem meschaunce!
Women and children of Sudan! Women of Colombia!
Kashmiri women! Punjabi women! Women of France!
Women of Britain! Women of Finland! Women of America!
They of Mecene leete enquere and seke
Of Lacedomye fifty maidens eke,
On whiche they wolden doon hir lecherye;
And foul delight.
Susters and nieces! Mothers aunts and doghters!
Deus Hic! God is drunk!

At these wordes words heven rose glood
the deepest soun son sound
a song sangen entuned intoned
a dense clamour clamor cries out
Love is leaving! the Earth quakes quaketh shakes under their feet!
some sort of deep tabour of drum or drone.
My tale is almost doon.
Some sawe some saying goes
some seyn some say
they say they saw des foules de crowds
en sang bleeding incensed, suster, the sky
is dreaming drumming up
red clouds of red blod an occean of blood ocean.
Amongst them they say they saw the joly Painter departed
swymmes floating, and all the time farting
in the hoote hot somer summer heat heete

with the glee of an Ashbery John.
Othere say that it was the old Papa's
body finally flying free
quit of its distasteful containee.
Here endeth the Franker Tale.

THE NOT TALE (FUNERAL)

The great labour of appearance
served the making of the pyre.
But how
nor how
How also
how they
shal nat be toold
shall not be told.
Nor how the gods
nor how the beestes and the birds
nor how the ground agast
Nor how the fire
first with straw
and then with drye
and then with grene
and then with gold
and then.

Now how a site is laid like this.

Nor what

nor how

nor how

nor what she spak, nor what was her desire

Nor what jewels

when the fire

Nor how some threw their

and some their

and their

and cups full of wine and milk

and blood

into the fyr

into the fire

Nor how three times

and three times with

and three times how

and how that

Nor how

nor how

nor how

nor who

I cannot tell

nor can I say

but shortly to the point

I turn

and give my tale an end.

FRIED TALE (LONDON ZOO)

> *Thereſ my tel*
> *Keap you wel*
>
> Riddley Walker

1

All juicit with an arseful of moola, wonga, clams & squids
doks stasht in identikl blakases hanging from ther hans
2 Suits, a mega pair of Smith, Blupils no dout,
viddying how they trading outa goodness welth stuporifik,
shake handes, hug n abuse ech othre on the bak.
It's a total blowout! we tawking millions a squilyons,
zilyons a nanilyons, bilyons a teramilyons
jus 4 kreaming the topping, o my brother.
Both tawk loudly in blinking err pieces
strapt in a same fashion Xaktly greyly a lykly
like goldnobs wanton be drest 2 a T like a G & G.
Roll in2 the glorious armpit of the worlds beestest whoring plugbord,
vastest Krystl struktur, bantring the bark off ech othre
speken cocktawk, wot bombdout area moostest reterns
wot lukered demolition wot goldn floodings
wot bestest crusading wot moostest profiteered!
Xlaff loudly, wot regionl blakouts,

wot farmakonikl funs, all in a days work,

brother deere, the worls our beetch wer getn a hed!

Entr the publik hostelrye 4 well-deservd drynk aftr the bauchery.

They go 4 strong wyn vino n setl down 4 som loud degobbing

ech latest local horrorshow. Well, says Smith, only last weke

I got an effing gr8 bubl outa som Ninja.

Wot in helle's Ninja? axes Smith.

Wostow you know, Ninja, no income no job no assets, responde Smith.

Tell tell! Xlaffs Smith.

Ok, says Smith.

Moost wynne if spareth nat, said I firstly to the Ninja.

Theres brass in muck, said I. Wel, not in so many wordes,

wots your leverage, I axd.

Ninja wer a tall 1, hansom and shiny with swet.

Im an athlete said Ninja.

Wel, said I, ure in chaunce, I said,

1 good leg is a v good start.

Ninja hesat one sek n an other very long sek.

By then wud drawn all contracted, all doks wer redy for bleading.

Fearing the worst, I grabit the lim at neejoint.

By the Flaming Ferraris, gimme here, its a good strong leg, said I.

Much bonding 4 this you wont regret, I said.

And I puld n I puld until the leg tor a way.

O my brother, twas a thing of bewt.

Ninja wer screaming, destackit on the flor

there was blod evrywhere

but funs wer releasing so fast
that all felt very satisfyngly w the deal.

I venturd, we eek hav wondrus stox
wot with 1 arm and a leg you koud elbo in2, venturd I.
Hell was popping that day. Doing bidness with this Ninja
was as blynly hot as smoaking up half of Hellas!
Coarse, said Ninja, rollit up a sleav.
We started cutting into the Ninja's arm dealings.
Soon afta the ymage of a seknd leg got floatit up
from the small kripply neighbour's printa.

A small partye of brethrens is now srounding the tallying teller.
By St Madoff! trupts a nother Smith larfing, lisning in.
Such are the great war wouns we see a roun these days,
continued I, you mited konsidr devesting
som of yr hi-risk relix into my hedge over there,
adventurd I to the Ninja, pointing somwere.
Wots that, said he, for wer a gready foole no dout.
Mobility skooter axesries.
I told im, werry nat n day, I said,
yr bidness will pik up, said I,
jus blead on the line, youl feal betere mediatly.
Coarse you stil have 1 good strong arm,
n wots priceless!

And this, my brothers, my brothers deere, sworne bretheren
that we are 4 as long as theres gold and silver in our cheste,
no bordas to our mathematikes, bidness cloking in as a grit
at 4 times the budge of public health, this o my brovas,
is how we got the sekond leg.

Feend lives in you, Xlaffs Smith. Wat genius strokit.
Less get anova such fino vinasse!
They pat ech ova loudly on the bank, lyte up cuba,
snort colombia, spray krystal all over the rest.
Suk on this bubl, from raiding to parading,
Im keaping it Im keaping it all! screachit Sir Smith,
1 publikly onurd feend of skotisk stox.
By the spans ov green expans, wot brilyant lyfe.
All larf n dig deepa in2 the publik kofins.

2

Amongst their noumbre besits one quiet felowe.
Prof. Galbraith is a very tall clerk, an economist w flair.
His son not so enkumberd whos made his phynance
pumping the Kurds but wots anova stury.
Givn his unusual height, Galbraith knows how 2 tell a good un.
Many peopl tel sturies n idle tels, som tru n som ovawise.
One kan spen the hoal lyfe-long with joy n sport in harping n piping
n other myrie tales. He trupts the party with this 1.

The newly started Banque Royale in Paris needed gold for its reserves. It hit on the idea that there might be some in the new American colonies although there was no evidence of the gold. Shares of the company were offered to the public. The response was sensational. The demand was high. Optimism built on optimism to drive prices up. A craze for junk bonds arose. It was wonderful. It saw some of the more riotous operations in all the history of financial greed. Selling and trading had to be moved to the more spacious Place Vendome. The amount of the coin that sustained the notes was soon minuscule in relation to the volume of paper. Here was leverage in a particularly wondrous form. Some being well received more were issued. People of all grades converted their property into cash and invested it in tulips. The wonder spread. Still there was no gold. It was no time for doubting. To maintain confidence and assure noteholders and investors that a goodly supply of the metal would be forthcoming, a battalion of Paris mendicants was recruited. The members were equipped with shovels and marched through the streets of Paris as though on the way to mine the metal in Louisiana. It was thought somewhat distressing when in the next few weeks many of them were seen back at their old haunts. It was no time for questions. All the predictable features of the financial aberration were here on view. When it came down all came down. The great speculation was coming to its unpredicted wholly predictable climax. Those who had contracted to buy at the enormously inflated prices defaulted en masse. Angry sellers sought enforcement of their contract. The courts were unhelpful. The notes were declared no longer convertible. The word panic as it pertained to money entered the language. Panic was total. Fifteen people died in the stampede. In search of milder less alarming reference: *crisis depression recession* and now of course *growth adjustment* came successively to denote the economic aftermath. French economy was depressed and economic and financial life was generally disordered. In the words of Saint Simon, a tiny minority was enriched by the total ruin of all the rest of the people.

Are u utrly totly lunatyke?
Wot kynde horse brayne spoile our cheery meal
terning the finest to vinaigret? The tenderest to leder?
What kynde vileynye be this?
Bedda watch your rot, mate, party kurly are smal tite circulars!
Xlaim the gorged gang of gogo boys pokit full of subs,
options, primes, bonii, bolly n I pass.

Well, continues the tall Professor, one thing certainly is. As the proverb has it, "Savit out some to keap in memberment that clevverness what made us crookit." Or as I wrote it in my *Short History of Financial Euphoria*: Financial memory lasts for a maximum of 20 years. This is normally the time it takes for the recollection of one disaster to be erased and for some variant on previous dementia to come forward to capture the financial mind. It is also the time required for a new generation to enter the scene impressed with its own innovative genius. Individuals dangerously captured by the belief in their own financial acumen and intelligence convey this error to others. Individuals and institutions are captured by the wondrous satisfaction of accruing wealth. The illusion of insight is protected by the public impression that intelligence of one's own and that of others marches in close step with the possession of money. We compulsively associate unusual intelligence with the leadership of the great financial institutions. Accordingly possession must be associated with some special genius. This view is reinforced by the air of self-confidence and self-approval that is commonly assumed by the affluent. An income of $550 mil was thought appropriate compensation for so inventive a financial figure. $8.5 mil was thought appropriate for resigning from a failed assignment of public proportions. The more the money the greater the achievement. On all these matters a more careful examination a sterny detailed interrogation to test his or her intelligence would frequently and perhaps normally produce a different conclusion. The circumstances that induce the recurrent lapses into financial dementia have not changed in any truly operative fashion since the Tulipomania of 1636. Even the Bubble Act of 1720 could not prevent the next one. Clearly the speculative episode is within the market itself. Markets being sacrosanct, clearly such a thought is unacceptable. It is necessary to search for external influences. The least important questions are the ones most emphasized: What triggered the crash? Were there special factors that made it so dramatic? Was regulation insufficiently relaxed? Who is to blame? There will be talk of regulation and reform. What will not be discussed is the speculation itself or the aberrant optimism that lay behind it. The euphoric episode is protected and sustained by those involved to justify the circumstances that are making them rich. It is equally protected by the will to ignore, exorcise or condemn those who express doubts. The only remedy is an enhanced skepticism that would not associate intelligence with the acquisition, deployment and administration of large sums of money. Between

1992 and 2007, the market grew by 150 times. As Charles Mackay wrote, nobody blamed the infatuation which had made the multitude run their heads with frantic eagerness into the net held by scheming projectors. These things were never mentioned. Frederic Lordon, economist, notes on his blog that in France today, salaries between a low-level operative and an executive already at a ratio of 1 to 30 are now in the region of 1 to 300. The Greeks called this pleonexia.

Let's assume there are no more than 24 accountable hours in the day. Let's assume that big patrons work for the eight prescribed hours. That they work for the following 16 hours too. Even if they work three times that of an ordinary worker and never sleep, the dilated bonanza superaddition cannot be accounted for. That's if we're calculating quantitatively. A leap is needed. The accounts must be calculated vertically, qualitatively. Then we see very clearly that the executive's time is of far greater intrinsic value (*d'une essence supérieure*) than anyone else's. It also makes much more sense, numerically speaking.

1 1 1 1 1 1 1 1 1 1 1 1 1 1 1
1 1 1 1 1 1 1 1 1 1 1 1 1 1 1
1 1 1 1 1 1 1 1 1 1 1 1 1 1 1
1 1 1 1 1 1 1 1 1 1 1 1 1 1 1
1 1 1 1 1 1 1 1 1 1 1 1 1 1 1
1 1 1 1 1 1 1 1 1 1 1 1 1 1 1
1 1 1 1 1 1 1 1 1 1 1 1 1 1 1
1 1 1 1 1 1 1 1 1 1 1 1 1 1 1
1 1 1 1 1 1 1 1 1 1 1 1 1 1 1
1 1 1 1 1 1 1 1 1 1 1 1 1 1 1
1 1 1 1 1 1 1 1 1 1 1 1 1 1 1
1 1 1 1 1 1 1 1 1 1 1 1 1 1 1
1 1 1 1 1 1 1 1 1 1 1 1 1 1 1
1 1 1 1 1 1 1 1 1 1 1 1 1 1 1
1 1 1 1 1 1 1 1 1 1 1 1 1 1 1

It means the desire to have more, to have more than one's share, to have it all. It speaks of a kind of mental instability, a terrible sickness that overtakes a person. Or a system.

Here endeth this grim detail.

3

Is that it?!

Xlaims somone way outbak from a sea of blu flikring lights.

Slipry fraternals dispers in the upstream

w relix handshakes n good vinasse

n we just go down w that?

Take murder for suicide

n we just go down w that?

Like fistfuls of hair puld out of social fabrik

Like disgarded chiken bones litring the streets

SO MANY THINGS IT GET ME ANGRY

SO MANY THINGS IT MAKE ME MAD

I GOTTA SAY AY

Like it says in the olden tale

Let the devils ass swallo em all

May they swarm inside his XL anal heat

Beneath his devils tail a hive of bloated brovas

a gobled nest of twenty thousand trapd freres in this place!

I GOTTA SAY AY

We're turning so mad

The place is turning so bad

Have my peoples live in fear n misery

All them people who hold them keys

I guess it come in like a judgement sign
the people have killing on their mind
SO MANY THINGS IT GET ME ANGRY
This place is a total disgrace
Too much pain
Theres too much pain
I wanna know I wanna know
SO MANY THINGS IT MAKE ME MAD
IN THIS BABYLON IN THIS LONDON ZOO

The partyes shokd, look up from their glas, skin is melting off their backs.

A great airwave battle looming for long on the floor now breaks out in the mind. Released by raggas crunched up bionic gyrations & the thug-steps beat bombs of ghosted out punk alliances. A wild grind-core sonic fire rage rises and envelops the senses, ignites enough basement anthems to exhaust the echo chamber, suk the air out of this terrifying hellhole with merciful subtronic nasty freqs liberation trail-outs.

The first and last dream warriors get to it by breaking down & restructuring cellular matter thru vibe circuits. Meshwork vibratory NRG that unpacks memry lockage and releases love-patternd terrains thru sonic shok. Drifts of clanging buzz. Smokes of haunted vocal fuzz.

Dead nerves.

Remedies suck.

Here for the game.

Dont follow the script.

Kick in the head.

Shit in the verse.

Revving reverse.

Enough fear. Enough greed.

Get out of this skin.

Out of this Bablon. Out of this London Zoo.

4

Last order! The bell goes.

We're in the Tabard, in the Belle, in the Cat and Fiddle, in the George and Pilgrim, in the Star and Eagle, in the Cock and Bull, in the Rose and Crown, Dame Justice is sitting on her arse, tis a pretty arse, downing a few. She's long since pawned her sword and scales to a broker. The only thing she does make a fuss about these days is the state of her beer. Like most ale drinkers, she doesn't like her beer cold nor with too much head. Big head has always caused controversy in Britain. Most beers have a small head but again these things vary. The very slow creamy froth of the Guinness and the way it sticks around is obviously unusual. If brewers generally regard it as part of the pint, an organization such as the Campaign for Real Ale ("campaigning for real ales, pubs and drinkers rights since 1971") argues that a pint should be a full pint of beer. Professor Srolovitz, mathematician, has found, that it's all to do with the density of the beer bubbles. "What happens in beer is the small bubbles shrink; the big bubbles grow. Eventually, the big bubbles pop. On Earth, there's gravity and the liquid that's within the walls tends to drain out back into the beer. The walls get thinner and thinner and eventually they pop". Beer foam is a cellular structure comprising networks of gas-filled bubbles. The speed at which the walls of the bubbles move is proportional to the curvature of the bubbles, and the duration and amount of froth settling on the top can increase as a result.

Dame Justice no longer worries unduly. She has a top up when needed. No longer gives a smiling sod about the moral attributes or social benefits of equitable share-out of wealth; or land; or health; or education; or how to work out well-being for the mostest; or the bestest ways of valuing peoples' skills or establishing fair and durable structures; or thinking long term; or facilitating technological access; or revisiting the rules of international exchange; or the balance of import/export; or the value of local trade; or determining the boundaries between life and death; or between breathing and unbreathing; or feeling and unfeeling; or animate and inanimate; or how to get out of the deep labyrinthine social moral spiritual physiological bankruptcy engineered by the brutal omnipathological so-called transnational trafficking bloodsuck oilsprung hyperdfunded plunderterprize. Sgot to be said she can be pretty longwinded. Speaks in sub-sections.

1a. Must fall. 1b. Should fall. 2a. Could fall. 3a. Will fall.

Along with the gigantic weather patterns, and poetic resistance now burning up nothing but its own cars, Dame Justice's done carrying the torch. She's wearing a costume of rickety splendour like a bridal warrior straight out of *The Last of England.* Emprisoned memories prowl through the dark, ah fuck it, they scatter like rats. Dead souls rat a pat. Armies move in. A patter. At any opportunity. Block the airports with tanks. Cars blow up. MOVE BACK. Stations close down. So many laws so much secrecy. Loose crowds. Cities on fire. Fire rising like tidal waves. MOVE BACK! Love elementals. Faces close-up. Everything burns. Lovers will always meet in the ruins, sleep and fuck amorously. Two lovers roll on the stretched out national flag and groan. Their juices will meet the rising waves of life's absolute crystal. Walls must fall eventually against the tide. Will fall. In the eventuality that walls could fall will fall. Must fall. To the elements. I've given my life once too many continues Dame Justice. Who will die again be slain again. Nobody listening nobody listening.

This time it seems we all go down together.
(Dame Justice looks up at the angry sun.)
Last order! Last order! The bell goes repeatedly.
Here endeth the Fried tale.

FIRST TAKE, TRACK ONE
(Roberta Flack can clean your soul — out!)

bass drums piano SAIDA LOVETHELIE bass LIETHELOVE bass HANGINON
bass WITH PUSH AND SHOV piano POSSESSION IS bass THEMOTIVATION
bass HANGIN UP bass THE WHOLE DAMNATION bass LOOKSLIKE piano
WE ALWAYS END UP piano INA piano RUT bass TRYINTOMAKEITREAL horns
BUT **COMPARED TO WHAT** horns piano drums bass

bass cymbals SLAUGHTERHOUSE bass IS KILLING HOGS bass cymbals
TWIST ED CHILDREN ARE KILLINFROGS cymbals drums POOR DUMB
REDNECKS ROLLINLOGS piano TIRED O LADIES ARE KISSIN DOGS piano
bass AN I HATE THAT HUMAN LOVE piano THATSTINKINGMUD piano
piano TRYINA MAKEITREAL horns BUT COMPARED TO WHAT horns bass

piano bass cymbals SAIDTHEPRESIDENT bass HES GOT IS WAR bass
FOLKS DONT KNOW bass JUSTWHATITSFOR piano bass NO ONE piano
GIVSUS piano RIME OR REASON piano YOUHAVE ONE DOUBT piano THEY
CALLIT TREASON bass piano I SAID WE'RE CHICKEN piano FEATHERS
piano ALL horns WITHOUT ONE GUT horns bass TRYIN horns MAKEITREAL
horns bass piano BUT COMPARED TO WHAT horns bass

drums bass piano cymbals GO TCHURCH ON SUNDAY bass cymbals
drums piano SLEEP A NOD bass TRY TO DUCK THE WRATH OF GOD bass
piano PREACHERS piano FILLIN piano US WITHFRIGHT piano TELLING
piano WHAT HE THINKS piano IS RIGHT piano cymbals WELL HE MUST
BE piano drumroll SOMKINDOV piano STUPIDNUT piano cymbals drums

piano HE TRIES bass T MAKE IT REAL drumroll piano TRY T MAKE IT REAL
YEA piano drumroll TRYIN TO MAKE IT REAL REAL REAL drumroll bass TRY
T MAKE IT REAL piano drumroll REAL REALYEA horns horns TRA T MAKE
IT REALYEA horns piano REAL REAL REAL REAL horns TRA T MAKE IT REAL
horns TRYIN T horns MAKE IT REALYEA piano piano

bass cymbals BUT WHERES THE BEE bass AND WHERES THE HONEY piano
WHERES MY GOD AN WHERES MY MONEY bass UNREAL VALUES bass
cymbals CRASS DISTORTION drums drums UN WED MOTHERS drums
drums drums NEE DABORTION drums AN IT KINDOV BRINGS TO MIND OH
piano YOUNG KING TUT piano HE bass TRIED horns TRIED horns TRIED
drums horns TRIED horns TO MAKE IT REAL horns drums cymbals TRIED
T MAKE IT REALYEA horns bass BUT COMPARED TO WHAT piano

bass cymbals SAID LOVE THE LIE L IE THE LOVE HANGIN ON WITH PUSH
bass AND bass SHOV bass POSSESSION IS THE MOTIVATION bass cymbals
HANGIN UP cymbals THE WHOLE DAM NATION drums LOOKS LIKE WE
ALWAYS END UP IN A bass RUT bass drums TRYINTO MAKE IT REAL horns
BUT COMPARED TO WHAT horns piano piano bass cymbals drums piano
bass piano drums piano bass piano drums piano piano

F U S E S (after Carolee Schneemann)

SOUND sea rush PINK FUSES
by Carolee ORANGE with herself *jamestenney 1967*
RED GREEN *glistening mouth cock* RED *tree cat* Seasound RED
shadow RED Sea GREEN *bodies fall back* burnt film Sea legs run
YELLOW BLACK bushes trees girl runs shadow Close-up BLACK
RED SEASOUND *suck window* RED *cock suck* WHITE window
SEASOUND break seagulls Cockwindow mouthwindow WHITE

GREEN paintfilmcloseup cockpaint mouthchin BLACK SEASOUND
Handfingers seagulls BLACK GREEN leaves leaves trees Window
WHITEGREEN BLACK RED wall erect moves tree leaves PINK
BLACK leaves PINKface GREEN BLACK RED SEASOUND seagulls
Seapaint back seagulls WHITE GREEN skin paintstroke BLACK
SEASOUND seagulls hand GREEN bleached movement arm
REDglisten BLACK GREEN WHITE top RED glisteningtrees BLACK

SEASOUND close REDREDblurryArse anuscrackupside verticalarse
REDthighs*female sits* WHITE*Burnt* GREEN fingers RED paintcum to
left GREENWHITE handbreast REDface backleg RED SEASOUND
REDface moveGREEN pubeBLACK RED SEASOUND seagulls
fuckrhythm REDBLACK *fuckrhythm* RED BLACK Sea PURPLE
bleachedface RED*rhythm* BLACK SEASOUND GREENback rest burnt
film perforated BLACKpaint Perforated *Lie classical Stretchbody back*

male rest Sideleg restingWHITE Burnt film face hair close nippleEyes stars face BLACK lock face close-up grasses wind SEASOUND *she lies breasts back Stars face to camera* Break kiss clear smile *long* REDBLACK film Kissclear burntfilm WHITE breast upside down fuckrhythm show breasts burnt film SEASOUND RED shadow BLACK *outline* PINKbodySEASOUNDseagulls outline negative fuckrhythmotion BLACK spotpatches SEASOUND seagulls shapes

patches film streaked*negative*SEASOUND streaked *negative* GREENlines paint REDsoil GREENmoves *background* BLACK Star holesFace GREEN cock GREEN leaves trees Vulva hairy bushy *seacunt* leaves PINKcock REDstones Blurry BLUEGREENcock right glisteningHandring finger pull cloth mate skinpube bushy *cunt tree* linesBLACK WHITE pubegoateeGREENcarGREEN BLACK flash WHITE glass GREEN face femaleSeakiss clear armBLACK hairface

Close fuckrhythm bleachedRED female face smiling burnt film PURPLE face smiling lying GREEN GREENface PURPLE GREENWHITEbodies SEASOUNDBLACKGREEN brow clear fuckrhythm rhythm underBrow Seaface fuzzeye closeupbleachedrest smokefacelyingpubecock RED paint lips Frowncunthairy REDWHITE nippleBLACKpube REDcatGREENseagullsREDcockglisten meat film *fuckrhythm camera smiles to camera* arm thighs arm thighs

caress R E Dcat boc cat arm *big red nipple* W H I T E   R E D B L A C K Sea
G R E E Npatchleft G R E E N R E D W H I T E G R E E N W H I T E nip R E D Arse
B L U E G R E E N   B L A C K pubeOpenperforated filmbreastB L A C K stop
filmG R E E N   W H I T E B L A C K R E D   S E A S O U N D Kiss B L A C K shadow
window shadow catarmkiss B L U E screen W H I T E window*Fingerhairy*
vulva swollen hairyswollencamera Window carry light window
bodymass *Standingfuckrhythm bodylock* R E D seagullsfingers B L A C K

cockglisten B L A C K R E D patch glisten B L A C K hair close Vulva close
hair B L A C K R E D Seaclose moves pulseR E D B L A C K B L A C K screen
R E D meat patches filmB L A C K cockhair ArmNail filmB L A C K W H I T E
R E D G R E E N film fullbodyG R E E Neyesface thinG R E E N B L A C K
SeaB L U E fullbody entwined faceBack B L U E G R E E N G R E E N W H I T E
B L A C K B L U E G R E E N B L A C K Sea W H I T E grasses G R E E N
white *cuntlick lieback* water lakefacethighs G R E E N entwined face upside

B L A C K P I N K G R E E N *bodylockface cat* G R E E N B L A C K move
G R E E N B L A C K Sea Sea B L A C K B L U E patch G R E E N streak G R E E N
B L A C K G R E E N leaves water B L A C K R E D lighttrees windowlight
G R E E N lights navelhair navelhair arm G R E E N turn navel hairy close
R E D cat wheel car treeslightbreasts smile light light trees G R E E N
still window lights O R A N G E window curtains Seacurtains
seagulls O R A N G E O R A N G E patches city Lightstunnel fuckrhythm lights

fuckrhythm steady *blowjobhairy fingersface* Seafuckrhythm
Down fuckrhythm lights BLACK WHITE BLACK waterwater
Sea suckfingers BLACK film BLACK fabric faces fabr
fingerBLACK GREEN faceGREEN Arsefilm CutRED finger face
WHITEfuzz arse fuckrhythm streaks filmBLACK film perforated filmRED
GREEN ORANGE fabric streakWHITE smile goateed legmuscle ringrest
stretch ORANGE Quiet slow arm *rest torn burnt film seagulls* sea arm still

GREEN female runs to sea arms Quiet seagulls arm sea arm still
RingcaressGREEN PINKstillSea female to sea waves GREENBLUE
runs to run seawalks to sea walks to sea walks to sea runs sea
fuzzGREEN superimp runstosea fuckrhythm runsback tocamera
swimwear to sea GREENfuzz runsbeach fillsRestlegRest
ORANGE window curtains curtains seagullswindembrace curtains
*brightdaylight curtains*window ORANGE gold SEASOUND BLACK

She's got wide creamy lips with stic
knots around the lips.

My cind such a nice list he v do
my st h y nanny molly. Sh an
report stroying their Barbies—for example, b d
th wing her head into the fireplace—as the on
My na y's got so n look hol
neve sticks out th ame

(To be a much travelled lollie d es
one can't fix one's lily). i

My slimy turf akes a nice green contrast to my dolly s

Sometimes my lollie pushes her doldo

My legs have many knots that tie me up in an ugly ball like a house of stress.

My dollie's such a nice dollie molly.

My dolly has many body parts. At night she pops... ushes

My cindy's got a big screw sticking out of her ... I twist her slowly into my dolly's arce when ever ...

In the morning when we rise it never matters what goes back on where. My dolly a good dollie She's got a wide satin slit down her lily for a

Sometimes my dollie doesn't work.

headless cindy to slot into.

My cindy has so many mouths my dolly never comes out the same way she in.

My doldo has lumps all over her plastic. It makes her look like a...

My doldo is My cindy's such a nice hairy dollie. She rides French be... for a headless cindy to slot into my safety nanny more than once a day.

For ... head, my daisy is a g... my mot daisy who pushes hers

My dollie is su My nanny's got so many holes ... once a day never sticks out the same way twice.

Yesterday my ... got her ... using until we re... with the lo... screw her top and oil it

My dairy's nose's so long no nanny can help sitting on it)

My ... tun makes My ... ollie's such a nice dollie molly.

She's got a wide satin slit down her lily for a she's got wide headless cindy to slot in ... ... ky... ushes her

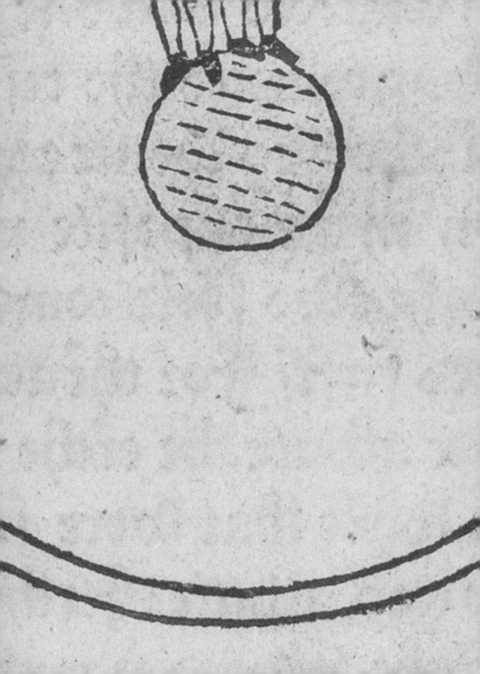

GOAN ATOM

(DOLL)

Our responsibilities did not begin in dreams, though they began in bed

Frank O'Hara

Arrhe est à art ce que merdre est à merde

Marcel Duchamp

Anybod's body's a dollmine

.   T   S

S   S   O

G   G   F

C   A   A

S   S   .

G   T   S

O   A   A

C   F   G

S

G

O

C

Enters the EVERYHOST
(dragging a badl Eg)
Finally!
So that the inspiration for such thoughts
becomes visible through the navel in order
To take advantage of the interior mechanism
run through the thoughts retained of little girls
as a panorama deep in the belly
revealed by multicoloured electric
illumination
it's roped in bottoms up I want to
B ba
b bo
b be
b leed
the load
o
Ff✶✶✶
Mud and Dead
the mud offal the dead
stuffed goat much
Junk & Gusto
Whats looking at me
Form Form Form
one hardened core after another
bleeding harp
PushPush Marquis

or Punch Olichinelle
Skin-sacks
Minor monticulates
lined Up joined by hind thoughts

OFART
Eat Shit gladly
both sides Atlantic
Forte love
Forte loot
o found ConCubicles
Some Fav affemmée
an Ourite's Belle
y firms ConCon
poupée de çuir poupée de çon
Cuillère des spoons orifficielles
the opening circa of my
Flask and Blood
(something outstandish about this bene
fits from micro friction)

Her e commaes
(such heir hair errs airs)

Enter DOLLY
Entered enters
Enters entered
Enter entre
En train en trail
En trav ail aïe
La Bour La bour La bour
wears god on a strap
shares mickey with all your friends

Sgot
a wides lit
down the lily
sgot avide slot
donne a lolly to a head
less cin
dy slots in

        to lic

Kher shackle
good dottersum
presses titbutt
on for the Puppe's
panoRama

nic
e round
ed olly

Woo pops
er
body partson
to the flo
ring the morning
it's never matt
ers what goes back
on w
here Dolly
goodolly
in a
ny shape or form

Wit one fine toast
erin the belly
wit no head
wit nos
ticky hairs
round the folly
and nof ingers at the tips
(or more)

All of LOL

LY's A FunC

they're full of joi
Hey full of joins
ke my dolly's knees t
Li

indy

likes hang
in
from the trees with
herl egs up in the air
egs dowhile her l
non
the ground

n

S

S

S

s

S

s pleine didely

Suc ha

clever holly
polie penny

sits on the cha
irk daisy
stickin gout
and a big bal
looms in the cranny

Wit ak not for the
hair sometimes blond
sum tied black again
st st
the wallpaper
or across
thes heets

Sgot uP
Elvis
(point to the Intero)
question mark

In a big way in
sclamation mark

Fact e's got
2
and a central boule

Shorts white ocks
end black shoes
for girls when e goe
> e goe Sout in the **woo**ds
> in the dark
> in a large coating
> Watch baby hind the trees
> P
> ouch
> contract a bunny ride
> on sweaty bice
> ickles your
> U C H hairy cr
> up

Still

a dirty doldo's

one fatpig

fruitcake

in the bowl of my pill

ow naughty bumps

ytrnally croks

my rip

the stickout grappe

of your naval ma d'olliv ery bad

storms today

very bad

DOLLY

Tank up !

This is the & of the world

                    T   S

                A

                F

Enter H E A D S T U R G E O N S
followed by
Enter F I S H M O N G R E L S
Colon speechmarks
Trouble in the Hous
?
illy all tied up

Nothing random
says the E V E R Y H O S T
about the herrings of this
fanny face
Once remove
able envelope
just stamp
or aply
anywhere
twice culled more lovéd

All presently engage in a
(vigorous)
POINT-DE-DEUX

What of it
bodymass is heavily funded
Swirling aHeads
roll out of place
mount alterity
part on display
round up
to as perfect a square as Octopus
ever canned

be
roll on roll on
MOTion
begs out of
g
GA
g
ging
Dis
g
orging
b
loo*
p
uke
s
uck
ack
ock
s
OG
ex
Creme
ental
eaT
ing sp
Am
mon
Am
mon
sp
you

d out
the 1 called
and one called
wholly
quartered
Beloved
Beloved
chok
en the Egg
SP
in
your arm
to ram
my Hoop
of larm
b
(click)
look
!
You Yo
footy
facey
click
yoyo
and a leg loops
into the
BAC of the
thRoat
and Ro
und and Ro
und and the Rolling Eye up we gl gloue
in the bl**dy dans hole

UNICA-HOUSE
(Homage Louise Bourgeois)

"consequently

it was necessary to spend some time in the vaults of the head

because that is where the fever really

c

omes to fruition

"

CINDY UNTIED #250

Bah Bah
By ba
Ba by
Baby a-hole is some
fairground to limins as these
easy not to know
which is when
& where is which
before in after-breach
Baby baby
catch your
skin a collateral
screwed into one sprawled
live-sized granpa
with a liver no
blood pud
no
rganic drill
do up e's mule

Never make dolls
full st
upscales
A CO CALLED MOO
Dolls should be seen full st
They should be gathered op op
They should be op With all my
H
H
eart

Lifting a large coming
into this massive evide
dented continues

Outspell each one of my sweet fear abouts
crossing the
BIG TOE
of Battle
sclamation mark

DOTTER
warf warf laffing
sucking on Lolly
swings a medoly

Mater Regina
was my first kiss
not my 2nd
yet the shadows flourish

Mater Regina
was my First V
not my third
nor my 4th nor my 5th

Mouth in a mool
Mool in a bloom
Mater Regina
was my first gash
not my last

(sudnly arosed exclaims)
NO
workable pussy
ever was su
posed to discharge at will
all over the factory
sclamation mark

AH YES

puts in the EVERY HOST

but sheeped

like a dolly

part out part ed

partout prenante

every little which way

right through the mid-

Come 'n

gain a bit

Come a kiss

(is made of this)

: it's a girl

Come a kiss

: and it's not

In fact it was

inconvenient

colon italics

Come again a bit freddy

said Anne listlessly

Nov 18 1819

to mate a door

in creset drawers

turn & turn the public lays

It must be humbly AD-
Mary by the lake
had a good
idea that is
"by some law
in my temperature"
quote MITTED invention does not consist
in cric-crac
crr crr
ee
a ting out of void
but out of the ka
bone of insecting
rooms unquote

Meaning comma
if we be wet in church
my swet inventory
hol da
headup inflate
my lily pousse my bridal suite
every mouth is ador
every little blood
draws
out another
casing

Blt **o** by bolt
Every single P
art is a crown
to Anatom

Loose all the parts
will have a funded funk

Doll y had a gold gueule & a belle mine

Throws up in the air
turns a pack of light
into a kit of bloodbone
A rouse! These crops

Fan out
aslow assem

Press out theYe
loocked up in kyhole
of this pandOrama

& the Mouth sHits out th Eye
Ambient Eye Amphibic Eye surRound

A very slow dissem
qui saime d'issem
assem d'issembl

shits th Egg in th Eye
Eye under Skin
press out
fan out

& the Mouth shits th Eye
Pun sPinning
in my Poussy Yolk
and my Hoily Boule

jette jets P
youpee splattering abouts
the b**ody study of a sacred pear

DOLLY (in bits)
Let Theart bod y M !

& **THEARS** clickage & The ighs come to.

S

A

G

Abodys a corps
Abody sa corps is cur bed
lie in it

says the EVERY HOST
For whom still sleeps encore in bod
in your bed Y vient in corps
Make fl
esh sometimes much agreed
encore encore!
in corps accord
mate loot with loot

Yet mostly corps à corps
loot mate with mate
A corps is a unit a detachment
a body's a corps disagreed
corps aggravé
tiréd in the flèsh

Also a detachable unit
aggrieved pried open
bloodied at corps
in bled in crops
then left for d**d

Unearthed
then stuffed for gain
If only bodied
and stuffed with fear

& the d**dman cRied as was laid to rest
who bled ry
pulling on this tired fleece

Time again
temps for the body of un corps

For the corps of a body body
For the body of a bod
Y bod Y bod

For a bod makes corps
not abode
Yet in body
Yet uncorps aboding

Uncorps d'encore
Un corps des corps
decorpsed décorps
decamps
échancre et d'encres au ventre
ride ride
for a being time another walkabout

A tabled GROUP OF CORPOREALS
Fitscrewed facial sites
Big coily brains
throbbing ambient genitals
swooning in cans of fish
swap heads all sitting on long brooms couldn't agree more
colon speechmarks
"Th brood would be swept clean out"
"Sweeping the brood clean out"

Blood has been wept off the lot
Pear-shaped machineries
that cruise one another's defaced milkmachines
slip on a slap on a Chatte Cat upfront
to sleep with Broad Loot
Outbroads La-Bonkings
Hefty lab onktonk ad hoc rigged up
shag the rut all butts too shine
fruit heavy a collection of holes
Bafr to ckont indifferently hanging at one an other's throat
Meatpunk! Gargoyle! Dirdymuƨƨel Brandmaƨƨ! Membrine Upmuƨhdbodglov!
Horrible languages outcries of woe
accents of anger Voices deep and horses with hands
smut together that swelled the sound of
the tumult through that air with solid darkness

I'm still bringing them through gently
says the EXPRESS COACH
I expect them to train as hard as I did
but they can't because their bodies aren't
ready for it yet
Compact jars of body conc
Crack op

–Entrate SLOB
w/ corporeal entourage
teeth hanging by the crowns
Boof boof speaks
des trous des airs des enfilades
half-wriggle half-hook
half-spittle
at the limits of perusal
Des compressions
Des arrois
Rejects of form
Oratorical bypass colon
Mankind, that's me
sclamation mark

Peak at twenty odd
Lean on facts in favour in cited
Hold on to pRoven limbs when hitting on
drifting object mater

RELAX

Permutate activating the lever vibrates right into the skull
provides very large w
inks anks

Eat change
Peer litter
Say Mma
Say Ppa
Spend the rest of this waking life catching up as in
poking faeces with a stick

WHY does filiation impress us so quote unquote
The supposition is that the oldest (sens du mot) is the nearest to truth
Or recalls what has been lost

All in all move about en mass
Best not to go it on one's own
One bad swipe leaves me to be disgussed

Some double-headed
In charge of sofening landscapes
t ween th dead the live the 10-digitalisd
Conversit in landing pouches:
"What drives a half-leg?
"There's hairs on that calf!
"Needled through one by one must

"Likelihooded!
"I want some!
"?
(verisimilitude)

And each one by one
Gober that one up

Wipes a good few
c
lean out of the Ff
rame Jump!
(I was pushed!)
fall out of the flot
into a collectively blank

Get-Off

Bang Bang the Bell
Y goes pop incessantly

Day in day out
the sound of bon hitting hom
limns itching each rep: eatedly: resented
Dup onder licate at will
Air compacted for ays and eeks
boom blows up the bloody mooning
from the mid out

THE ARTIST
as archivist as archaeologist as bricolist as cataloguist
as collatist as collectist as compilist as ethnografist
gathers up the debris particles
as residues as indices
hung from wire
lit from centre

A SCALE OF TEATS
(14 juicy and penetrating in all things)
Alloy
Alloy
The spc is full of slosh and form

(praise knees d)

Enter clac-clac clac-clac
CHORUS A SCHOOL OF TEETH
head for a croupe
and a croupe for a neck
speechmarks
Nothing can compare
to te icdil of body past
humanolo clac
crowded physiques wat mumbl "vaseline"
and mount one a noter's rising
melanclac cholia

MERCHANTS
Fuck skin
The ternal is urgical
Is the ternal urgical
Animated turn
tables patent Ason
from a boxo orgns

A SCHOOL OF TEETH
Icdils of summer clac
Fish are flying
and te living is easy
Lazy pick-nooks in
te fat green of feels
clac postules

MERCHANTS
We're not acturally
against skin
worn long in season

ALL PRESENTED ream on one elbow

Praise knees d
Praise knees d

One elbow
to elbow
b-
ack to

(ife)

th absent Loeuf – that merry L-ip

breaks off the cuff
intones an opera
tive moutful
flayed lengthwise

Ambient fish fuckflowers bloom in your mouth
Ambient fish fuckflowers bloom in your mouth
Ambient fish fuckflowers bloom in your mouth
Ambient fish fuck flowers bloom in your mouth
Ambient fish fuck flowers loom in your mouth
Alien fish fuck fodder loose in your ouch
Alien fish fuck fodder loose in your ouch
Alien fuck fish fad goose in your bouch
Alien phock fish fat geese in your bouche
Alien phoque fresh fat ease in your touche
Alien seal fresh pad easing your touch
To fish your face in the door
a door a door
fuckflowers bloom in your mouth

will choke your troubles away
will choke your troubles away
will choke your troubles away
will shock your double away
will soak your dwelling away
suck rubble along the way
suck rubble a long way
suck your oubli away
watch a getting a way
watch a ramble away
take the gamble away

will choke your troubles away

Ambient fish fuckflowers bloom in your mouth
Ambient fish fuckflowers bloom in your mouth
Ambient fish fuckflowers bloom in your mouth
Ambient fish fuck flowers bloom in your mouth
Ambient fish fuck flowers loom in your mouth
Alien fish fuck fodder loose in your ouch
Alien fish fuck fodder loose in your ouch
Alien fuck fish fad goose in your bouch
Alien phock fish fat geese in your bouche
Alien phoque fresh fat ease in your touche
Alien seal fresh pad easing your touch
To face your fish in the door
ador ador
fuckflowers bloom in your mouth

will choke your troubles away
will choke your troubles away
will choke your troubles away
will shock your double away
will soak your dwelling away
suck rubble along the way
suck rubble a long way
suck your oubli away
watch a getting a way
watch a ramble away
take the gamble away

choke your troubles away

ALL PRESENTLY
have never felt so close to wanting a
Heart to boot
is fast becoming
the latest continent around

DOLLY
Kss my fr
og
ock
Rub the genie tales
Some dream off kin
for kind
want a better make
another and-and
and and and and
"finely structure mesh"
"suitable scaffolds"
seed a kleenex today
to marrow the world
much like
"growing an arm and hand"
mol assumule eculargesse
bandaged on
not born slurpy
quote Someday Independent
22 Feb 1998
"The hurdle is nerve tissue"

Much in it who saw som ingle with Postfaced
dotted in small groupings
mooch about mocks a Vie
Garbs root garbs for routes

workit baby

And the spac eB ween's solids
& the spac in solDis peed s Peech

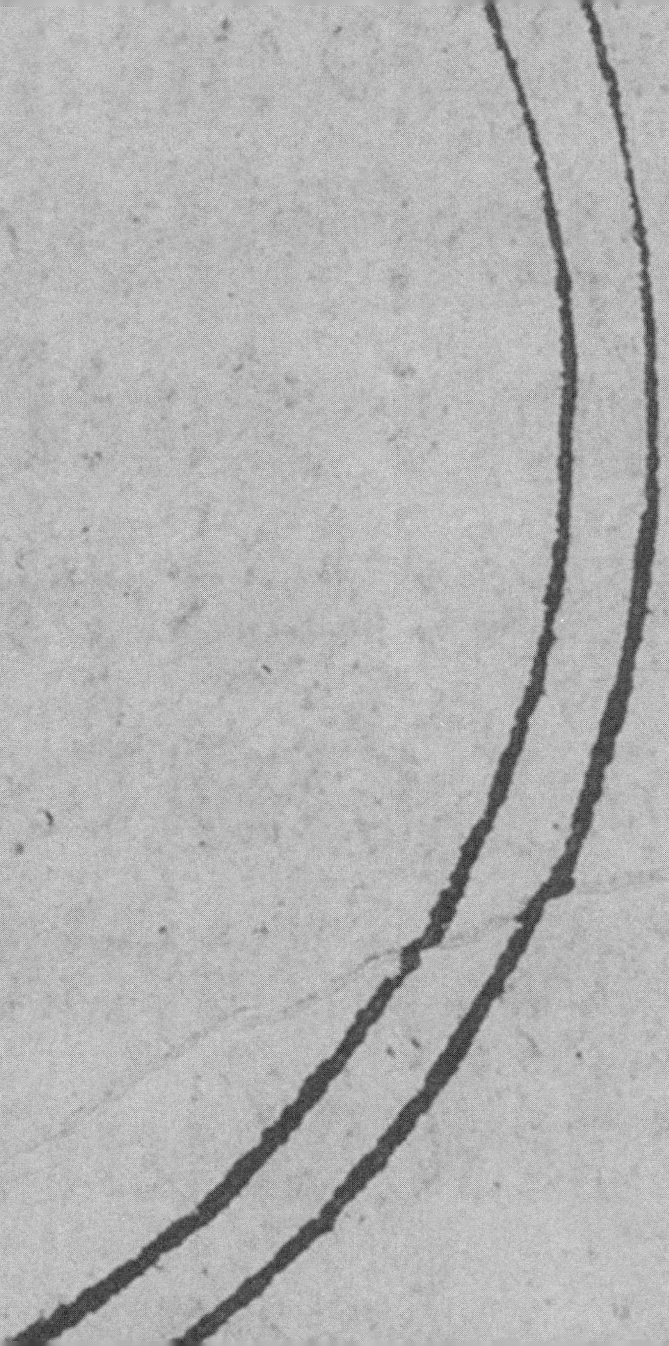

U N T I T L E D (homage Inger Christensen)

I keep on my desk a small jade uroborus given to me a few years
back. The jade is dense and brownish. The object is nearly flat and
beautifully carved on both sides with stylized geometrical marks.
A few rounded lines make out the elongated head. There's a small o
for an eye carved on either sides of the head. There's a small
papertag hanging from the object: "Warring states 6-10 AD." But is
this a 2 or a 6 or a 16 or a 4 or a 14? Does this read 12-16? The Chinese
Warring States (480-221 AD) refers to the period of wars between
seven major city-states, that led to the creation of the first Chinese
Empire. It was also a time of great intellectual ferment. It gave rise
to Confucianism and Taoism. It announced the spread of literacy
outside of court circles. When the Han family took over the newly
created Empire of Qin, it made sure to restrict access to manuals of
military and political strategy that could foment revolutionary
ideas and tactics, such as Sun Tzu's *Art of War*. The Han Empire
conquered, revolutionized social structures, imposed its own
system and language, became the world. Eventually fell, collapsing
on its own greed.

There are paths that should not be taken.
There are forces that should not be confronted.
There are fortified areas that should not be attacked.
There are situations that should not be contested.
There are rulers' orders that should not be accepted.

The uroborus's tail fits neatly and effortlessly inside its mouth as uroborus' tails do. The head of the uroborus cannot stop eating the tail, the tail of the uroborus travels down its own body in reverse direction. This feels uncomfortable, and that is perfectly normal. It feels strange, as though the tail was somebody else's, yet when the head bites its tail, it hurts, and that's a good sign too. All is as it is, and while the uroborus spins, it never begins, it is always in motion. If the mouth were to become suddenly greedier and stronger, and the tail were to loosen its resistant grip, it would all take a different course. The mouth would eat its way unimpeded all the way back to its own mouth. The whole in the middle would disappear. The uroborus would become a tiny compact sphere, and finally explode from its own pressure. Or if the mouth were to release its grip, the tail would shoot out in a flash, like an arrow, a fully extended snake, and disappear out of sight. A spark of fire created by the unstoppable friction would light up the entire body and turn the vast mechanical zero to ashes. Filling the hole with another substance so as to prevent rotation, would implode it and transform time as we know it. For now, it has caught itself by the tail. It has fallen into the mathematical hell of infinity. It is a sign that all is as it is.

The hole in the middle is wide enough to put one or two fingers through. The jade stone of my uroborus takes on the cold, rugged feel of lizard skin. The rules of love are rules of battle between matter, within matter and beyond, in which beings blend, in which bodies exchange strength and suppleness, fluids and depth. Roles become interchangeable. Social body grooming for sex is carefully taught, sexual and erotic variations trained up. Repetitions are frequent. I own a cheap copy of the *Kama Sutra*. Its translation by Danielou delights in emphasizing the liberatory potential of skillful sex. Skillful gender proliferation. When a peak of pleasure is attained, internal and external worlds disappear. Repetitions are frequent. Repetition can lead to release.

There are sixty-four elements in loveplay prior to copulation. It is claimed that the preliminaries to sexual intercourse involve sixty-four elements, probably because they were originally described in sixty-four chapters. We repeat this figure because in the opinion of old, the ancient treatises had sixty-four chapters. According to certain authors, it is the body of erotic treatises that is divided into sixty-four parts.

Following a structure, one enters another.

ABOUT FOAM

A paradoxical pleasure is both solid nor liquid that can be wet, dry, hard, soft, expansive, changeable. An intricate and hollow polymer network is energy transport at its finest, a compound structure of gas nor bubbles nor fans. Once hardened it can be tough to break. What binds. A gel for instance can envelop like an elastic skin. It can be prodded distorted pushed about, yet will bounce back and hold its shape. Under greater surface tension, it breaks into liquid starts to flow. A resilient responsive substance is mysterious, swift to morph, ever present in all that is cellular and delivers a shake-up. It supports the many invisible synthetic demands of industry-dependent living from insulants to binding agents. It has naturally assisted in the solidification of soap, the rising of bread, egg whites, and soufflés since the 17th century. The old ponce pumice stone works on hard callouses. Once exploded it can be hard as ash. The skeletal containers of dead sponges were used by Romans for brushes and combs, and for cups. Proust's memory work is foamic in a foam-lined room. A sudden foaming from the mouth for instance is the warning of miles of a thick sluggish matter heaped along coastlines, or bubbling up, obstructing the flow of vast indus-trial evacuation conduits. Matter turns unwelcoming, seemingly unrecognisable. A persistent reactivity to events in its surroundings acts on a profound imbalance, the sign of a system being worked beyond capacity. Foams everywhere like the letter e, down to the alveolar structure.

1.

Papyrus stems from a plant. A type of reed that grows along the bank of the Nile. One presses two opposite sides together perpendicularly and washes them down with mud and pounds and pulps them to create a thick, smooth and durable writing surface. Sheets of these papyri were used not only for writing but for wrapping the dead. In the cartonnage of an Egyptian mummy, the flexible layer of fiber or papyrus was moulded while wet into a plaster-like surface around the irregular parts of a mummified wrapped body, so that motifs could be painted on. Philosophical treatises, poetic pieces, dramas as well as bills, accounts, have been discovered around the mummies. Wrapping one written substance around another. Like newsprint around fish. Plant-pulp and animal matter.

At the end of his autobiographical work *Barthes by Barthes*, the writer chooses to feature a plate from the French philosopher Diderot's Encyclopedia. It is taken from the "Anatomy" article and is the 9th in a series containing in all 33 plates. This one represents the vena cava, and on this plate it looks suspiciously like a tree. The head is a bushy mess, the circuit channels are close to branches with leaves. At the end of his meandering work, Barthes turns his account to the botanical world of the human plant.

He doesn't structure his autobiography chronologically, but rather as a complex of substrates: personal sketches, scholarly jots, semiotic observations, encyclopedic illustrations, photographic documents, drawings, graphological traces. All topographic stimuli, tropisms of being.

He examines his body. "Which body?" he writes. "We have several."

Clarice Lispector's haunting novel *The Hour of the Star* is dedicated to what she calls "returning to the grass."

In Alan Moore's radical recreation, *Swamp Thing* is a human lettuce, a morphic transhuman vegetal entity, a large anthropoconscious plant, the result of a scientific experiment on a dead man, a plant elemental who "remembers having bones, and so it builds itself a skeleton of wood. It remembers having muscle and constructs muscles from supple plant fiber..." Swamp Thing returns to grass.

Sappho's love for a lettuce is only one episode in love's transmorphic capacities.

Although Diderot was one of the main proponents and thinkers of that intellectual and scientific ferment of the Enlightenment that dislodged Western humanity from its surroundings, it is worth noting that when it comes to sentientness, the philosopher was still wondering what the absolute difference between a plant and a mammal might be. In this, he found only matters of gradation.

2

bracket
bracket "gladness and"
bracket
(Fragment 20)

The poet-translator means to show us the archaeology of the poetic document, its initial material papyrological event, its written plant-state. She uses brackets to stage a connection between text and "papyrus dust." The brackets want us to imagine the corrosive dust, the holes, the rot, the degradation of the text's material support. They do not restore so much as materialize the ruin's cohabitation with the present.

The brackets do not sing and do not speak. They show and separate what's in from what's out, what's here from what's gone. They do not imagine the text that might have graced the vanished sections of scroll, they simply represent that something is not. The text's material history is allowed to resonate at the heart of the poetic work but as she comments, "to represent all the erasures would riddle the pages with brackets." One wishes she had. Why put some in and not the rest?

The success of a translation is its contemporaneity. In another epoch, the point would have been to fill in the gaps, to recreate the unrestorable, to avoid what cannot be controlled, to turn everything into language. Anne Carson's bilingual and bracketed translation of Sappho's lyric ardour makes it a poetics for our times, a language of the erased, of the stranger, of the visual stutter and the hyphenated or elliptical being. Of the co-existence of written and erased. Of verbal and visual. And also of the bracketed-out, phantasized singing voice in a silent and inscriptive context. Forever the rot will cohabit with the readable. The ruin with the erudition. The love with what's left.

But then Carson, in her introduction to *If Not, Winter* writes: "It seems that she knew and loved women as deeply as she did music. Can we leave the matter there?" Sure. But leave what matter where?

Sappho is compost. Sappho-compost. Not-papyrus to papyrus, copyists to printed page, wet burial to bodies to burning desire to song to musical instruments to language to fragment to perfumed clothes to poetic impositions to social silences to translation norms to literary formulae to erotic beauty to restorations to lovers to creations, part-noun, part-adjective, part-address, part-history, part-gossip, part-lyre, part-vegetable, part-sapphic. Precipitate. Or a punched score for mechanical piano.

The Japanese photographer Hiroshi Sugimoto reaches for a similar thought. His photographs of movie theatres taken during the full length showing of films reveal how the human spectators have all but been burnt away by the continuous exposure of his camera. How the movie houses in fact are only ever filled with radiance. How simply and totally human matter just vanishes into its own architectures, into its own material and technological structures.

3

In the press mid-Dec., one could read that the lasting shock for collectors of the Young British Art scene of the 90s is that a lot of this work wasn't "meant to last." No surprise there, but loud consternation that Damien Hirst's medicine cabinet should have started to give out a foul odor as the pills are fermenting. His shark in formaldehyde has already had to be re-stretched as the skin was starting to shrivel inside the faulty liquid encasement. Legal situations arise. "I looked at the Saatchi collection and you could see that the condoms on Tracey Emin's bed had become brittle – of course they have, it's almost ten years old. This raises the question: can these things be replaced? Will any old condoms do, or do they have to be Tracey's?" said one private collector to *The Times* (30 January 2007).

4

When it comes to paper, wood-pulp papers are inferior in almost every way to rag-based papers and to vellum, derived from animal skin. Laws passed by the British House of Commons are recorded and stored on vellum.

In his book *A Universal History of the Destruction of Books from Ancient Sumer to Modern Iraq*, the curator and conservationist Fernando Baez notes that "paper made of linen or cotton rags is durable, but the introduction of wood pulp and new bleaching and gluing processes brought with them unstable elements, such as hemicellulose and lignin." It is ironic that the savage industrialization and deforestation needed for wood-derived paper production in the mid-19th century, which to such an extent democratized the book and literary production, should be what is now also threatening the very existence of entire archives.

"Of the approximately twenty million books and pamphlets in the Library of Congress, approximately thirty percent are in such a critical condition that they cannot circulate."

The artist chooses standard paper sizes, at standard weights, printed using standard lithographic treatments, cheap photolabs. This work engages with the material processes of printing not through design and artistic production, but rather through expressly standardized processes from industrial or commercial printing plants. The Cuban-American artist Felix Gonzalez-Torres's well-known *Stacks* engage with low-grade material processes of mass-printing and mass-dispersal. He doesn't seek to produce work to high quality standards, standards that might ensure the preservation of the work and a slower rate of yellowing and fading. The industrial paper used for his posters is a lower grade paper than that used for books, and often bleached with chlorine. If it is not acid-free, as is necessary for paper intended to last, it quickly deteriorates.

Punters are invited to help themselves to sheets whenever a *Stack* is on display. Each is an extension of his arts activism as much as of his minimalist aesthetics. It reflects his suspicion at the immobilism of the art object and his own thinking about exchange and personalized artistic experiences. It propels his work towards an intimist if detached practice, one in which objects are signs and events, rather than things and collectibles, and where private events are represented alongside anonymized and collective ones.

Stack of white paper (endless copies) at ideal height 9"
"Untitled (Passport)."

Stack of blue paper (endless copies) at ideal height 7 1/2"
"Untitled (Loverboy)."

Stack of white paper (endless copies) w/ offset print of small B/W portrait pics
"Untitled (Death by Gun)."

Stack of white paper (endless copies) w/ offset print of news clipping: ATLANTA, MAY 24 – A lot has happened here since Joyce Simpson saw the face of Jesus in the forkful of spaghetti on the Pizza Hut billboard near Coleman Watley's Jiffy-Lube (recto)
"Untitled (Spaghetti)."

Stack of white paper (endless copies) w/ offset print of 2 identical touching circles
"Untitled (Double Portrait)."

Stack of offset printed paper (endless copies) of a B/W photograph of a luminous clouded sky
"Untitled (Aparicíon)."

Stack of white paper (endless copies) w/ offset print of news clipping: GIVE A CHILD A BREAK: GIVE TO THE FRESH AIR FUND (recto) and offset print of newsclip: Germ Warfare Research Safe, Pentagon Says After a Study (verso)
"Untitled."

Stack of offset print of black rim on white paper (endless copies) at ideal height 8"
"Untitled (Republican Years)."

Stack of offset print on red paper (endless copies)
"Untitled (We don't Remember)."

Two stacks of white paper (endless copies) at ideal height 26" each
"Untitled."

These pieces will survive by chance by accidents, a few sheets here or there, the randomness of someone's archives. The print will fade from the large printed paper work on my wall. How long will it take? A large grey sheet. It ties in with historical ephemera, transient documents of everyday life, minor documents such as labels, tickets, receipts, not adverse to but never intended for the surprises of mudification. It ties in with grassroot archives and the work these do to counter the under-representation of specific or local sets of social and material culture. It signals an intimate discipline, a rigor, a commitment to telling what is necessary, mysterious, shocking, pleasurable. Sharing one's traces and observations while disappearing, while being punched out. In very simple ways, but not simpler.

CROPPER

CROUP

Under pressure my hands sometimes balloon to the size of small
waterbombs, now that Ive been travelling across 8 time-zones,
havn slept in 26 hours or havn slept in 3 months, more or less since
receiving an invitation that had read, pls write a piece in
Norwegian. Can I do this, distanced for many years absented.
Very gradually I reach the conclusion that a bissextile year w its
intersticial day mite prove propitious to, as they say, emptying
ones bak, taking a long hard look at one selves—

Using the good fortune of the leap year, the intersticial day is one
for archives and time ajar, I decide to develop a nexus of drafts and
thoughts designed to prod or othrwise demonstrate the following
arrangement, a sketch, a portrait-outline of myslf as a bilingual,
binational, dispersd, ssipated, French hyphen Norwegian writer.
Someone bordering on, never settld, whos changed codes like coun-
tries in a free-to-roam White European fashion, not forcd to move
by politics or social circmstance, this being debatable at a psycho-
logical level, must move on can't move in, ever since I no longr
could write in French, having been caught off-guard by its le-la
structure, thrwn out of its crucial tra-la-la. This is how it happend—

She appeard to me frankly. Lifted me up from childhoods lipsings, showd me the field the dawn aurora thru the bursting green of the French valléy, all around the arbouring trees blind us w shards of verre in the light mounting silver birds slivering past. Voila she led me to the river, eau eau pressd me down lifted my long brass towards the seal of the summer sky, up-chemised my shirt peléd layers of cloth and peeling skin, couchd me safely profondly on this earth. Then placed a lump of saliva on my tongue and gave me language. Opnd the port to the door, the bush of the mouth bled me made me bleed, blood is the first song, traveld across me trawld me w fever. Fired me up w language. A splendid exacting luminescence to be sudnly awake in ones own language. I was awake in language. Vivid carcasses splayed out in the day solair, neither partial nor incomplete, neither left nor leaving, each in each contained and all subsumd in all. It wasn French what came thru French, not language as we keep it, yet came w language what came w her. Brightness dissipates our shapes to the weightlessness of burst conches—

To be made in one min in a single sec. To flesh out in one lettre then b torn to pieces by the next. Be seized as though lifted by an electrical storm, a prehistory of spines pushing out from within ones column, then see ones life tumble out. Swim in ones current, then b thrown on deck, wrung out to dry. Nonono came the voices choral came the law. Loud verbal hindrances, they tear through my mystries. Nono no body be languaged sexd in this way, a crowd moves in, anuls this ovr-exposure to light. Tear down subsequent years, reorganise my orgns. I lose my one, corps déserted, first language beatn out of it. How will I speak. One feels the need to allegorise, then came years of sorrow, hiding, interior struggle and spiritual misery etc. The next time I come round, Im mute, languid. Stilted stille from years of mouthing language w a mouth full of coins and stones. I pass into Norwegian, relievd if wary of a 2nd lang in ones stream, by now one knows policed behavior, the efficiency of home-monitring. How will I love—

Writing is a gesture across space, ski trails in a freezing landscape, a long brisk winter, en lang norsk vinter. Learn how to withstand the cold brings self-sufficiency to ones protective silence, every-thing controld to a level of quiet inactivity. Emotion gets toned down, distributed to favor regulated dormancy, isolation indext, waiting methodical. One imagines that in such an environmt, the catalepsy of xperience will start releasing vocab. It dosn work like this, tho provides room for maneuver. Uproot brings the spring. Uproot springs a lip. Friends bring a kitchen table, fresh food supplies, and sound equipmnt. Time to move. As of now all I am and all I do is accentèd. Best to speak while I can. Breathe while I breathe. At first my languages must b small and localisd, precise and tangibl. Tongues might splintr easily bween my teeth. Keep each detail, each cutting for a coming utrance. Deformd or misshapd souns can b held togther by hyphns, new clang b freely integrated in the lasticity of my livd self, a new stage, adopted and integrativ. Yes, an English familiar will do fine, it signs on easily, seems adaptiv, resonant, all steps made provisory to help shape ones physical and mental outpost, my linguistic physiology—

The journey across was not traumatic, only inr grooves throw a difrent line, from CDG to OSL to LHR w corresponding passprts, the gaps appear not at ntry, only w the passing years, I had imediately takn to Londons queer sensibilities w its enjoymnt of iconoclastic performance trads, trance hosts, and this large, ancient, encumberd city had seemed to take to mine, absorb me in2 her. Undr railway arches on the stages of late-nite clubs in flamboyant revampd Saf London pubs in the rooms of local performing arts venues in strange and claustrophobic poetry rooms, I coud pass for somone, b perfectly dismulated. Fan out, anglisize to fall in, take a place at the scene. In this new guise was founded, made articulate by a shared and amusd aquiescence to odd cadence, nu nude, the speaking insistens of lovers sticking on lipstick n tashes, artists hanging thick strands ov hair cross the doorway, feeling train vibrashns long the walls, near the heat ov the machine, flies foreigning, each of us at work—

Words r vibrations pattrns of activity, units prefigurd that steep us into prefab. Colour a reminder that beings n objects r vibrations in the end but vibration. Depth of contrast, intense attraction spred across our volumes. Terrible conflictual resonance xplodes in the outlines. Yet language perception begins as a sensation of structurd resonance, sounded air glottal vibration, rumord not pronounceable releases clusters of negative-space that shadow and trail this solid flask, these partly-nons half-theres, what are they. Residues, colorful earfuls, knots ov being, ghostings ov voices just past on the street or in the centry mysteriously sound out my own

changing substance, magnetic pleasure in aural landscapes, how
riting resumes a root—

Waking dreams change away from birth languages, become more
cautious yet paradoxicly wildr, harshr and more pragmatic.
Conditional, they demand othr skills. Misprnouncd words
somtimes freez up in-btween, dormant sphers intrud on the
trajectory of use, sudn trance-outs, panic not picnic, nit-pick this
packt launch, yet vertigo brings a relief, and relief. This linguistic
house is at anothr level from the sea. Th sentens flatns moralises
distances. Away from the fertile emotive chaos of words, buoys or
chains that drag ther anchrs along w miles ov algae, seapods n
crustaceans atasht. Furthr up along the citys flanks. From here one
can gage the fog. If the wether clears one can see the citys vast
industrious topography. Whenever I faultr I go bak to practicing
spitting, phonemes, pickled onions. Fear that I might lack the triks
to attent the trek, hooha of the assent to furthr verblization, the
range of distribution needed to steer a clear terrain, both to
ssimilate n dissemble, on a final count, to have exceeded my own
destination—

Its fair to think that whn one arrives to language fully grown, soms
past bodyshape will be left blissfully in the dark, that one can start
at anothr one. Perhaps one shoud have imagind that pleasures not
so botherd, that this body would lack most of the somatic and
cultural presumptions familiar to standard bearers of a language
and a country where daffodils are not so much spring flowers as
wandring clouds. Indeed how reliable was this light-headed

roaming, a state of cultural afazia, woud one have to learn to embed the nursery rimes, the cultral undrcurrnts and scaffoldings to signs n sense, create a developing infancy, a 3D spec of ones shape n skin, run thru by rivers undrground, always run thru, or could one simply forgo this 1 n carry on from a poetic imaginary eerily free of white rabbits doubld-up instead between unlikly Norwegian trolls and unrecgnisabl French childhood songs bout bridges n ladeez in medieval gardns—

Skin warps. Wraps around both injury and pleasure. Adjusts to any new bulk, tries to invent movment for itself. Deforms to absorb. Just as I thought I was atome, what is this, my hands r ballooning up, pulling upwards as tho trying to lift off, do we have lift off, dragd up by my wrists out of hide-out. For awhile I had mistakn my hyphn the dash of my cultures for a ful stop. I know I wished for this, to stop somwher. At last to stop at this, to hide on it, no longr looking out or following connections, no longr wishing to have it for a plunj, a real dive, jump from the springboard, the diving-board. Mentl discipline n critical forms of friendship, hyphended shapes drive the energy, summon up the terms, demand more perseverance. Like som seek in the transformative aspect of serial or patternd work a release from identity that is a release into motion perception, or in meditation traditions w their demanding refinements of posturs n mantras, a pathway from individual isolation to cultural engagemnt. Some compose a rugged syntax, a perturbd language that substantiates personal events w conflicted blonging, creases the bordrs, rules, boundaries, edges, limbos at historical breaches, reveal the depth of sedimentation. Some place their intellectual and poetic bodymass in such a way as to blok, resist bear witness to enforct forms of kinship. Force applied to language eradicates whole strands of individul n collective bodyshapes. Some apply them selves to electricity. Somthing did finally burst. Much points to where she left off, motion shadow, the ripple in the air that follows a jump, dive in the mid of the wired air, wake up mid-stream, wake up streaming, inside the skin, under the skin of my time—

CROP

How does one keep ones body as ones own, what does this mean
but the relative safety of boundaries, could I make sure that what I
called my body would remain in the transit from othr languages,
that it would hold its progression into English, and because I didn
know and wasn sure, and since for a great number of people, for an
overwhelming number of persons, for an overwhelmingly large
number of persons, for an always growing number of persons, this
is far from self-evident, this is not self-evident, this does not
apply, this doesn even begin to figure, I never knew for sure—

Some never had a body to call their own before it was
    taken away
som aldri hadde en kropp de kunne kalle sin egen før den ble
    revet bort
ceux dont le corps d'emblée leur est arraché

Some never had a chance to feel a body as their own before it was
   taken away
som aldri fikk oppleve en kropp som sin egen før den ble revet bort
ceux dont le corps d'emblée leur est arraché

Some never had a chance to know their body before it was
   taken away
som aldri fikk kjenne sin kropp før den ble revet bort
ceux dont le corps méconnu d'être arraché

Some were never free to speak their body before it was taken
   up and taken away
som var aldri frie til å si sin kropp før den ble løftet opp og revet bort
ceux dont le corps est arraché

Some tried their body on to pleasure in it before it was taken up
   beaten violated taken away
som tok sin kropp på for å nyte den før den ble løftet opp slått
   krenket revet bort
sont ceux au corps choppé violé arraché

Some had their body for a time then it too was taken away or
    parts of it
som hadde sin kropp i en tid så ble den også revet bort eller
    deler av den
sont ceux dont le corps n'est plus signalé comme l'un des leurs

Some thought they had their body safely then were asked to leave
    it behind the door or parts of it
som trodde at de trygt hadde sin kropp bare for å bli bedt om å la den
    bli igjen bak døren eller deler av den
ceux dont le corps emporté au loin des leurs

Some hoped they had one safely only to find it had to be left across
    the border or parts of it
som håpet de trygt hadde en kropp bare for å innse at den måtte bli
    igjen over grensen eller deler av den
ceux dont le corps à la frontière nié n'est pas des leurs

Some wanted to leave their body behind and couldn't
som ønsket å legge sin kropp bak seg og kunne ikke
ceux qui ne pouvaient pas

Some could neither take it with them nor leave it behind

som kunne verken ta den med seg eller legge den igjen

s'y prendre s'y laisser

Some bodies are forgotten in the language compounds

Some immense pressure is applied on to the forgetting of the
    ecosystems some escape from

Some bodies like languages simply disappear

noen kropper liksom språk blir simpelthen borte

disparaissent comme les langues

Some or many are being disappeared

noen eller mange er blitt borte

ont été disparus

Some or many disappear

noen eller mange blir borte

sont nombreux disparaître

Some or many that disappeared arise in some or many of us
noen eller mange som ble borte reiser seg i noen eller mange av oss
disparaissent se lèvent en certains de nous

Some arise in some or many of us
noen reiser seg i noen eller mange av oss
se lèvent en nombre de nous

Some that arise in some of us arise in many of us
noen som reiser seg i noen av oss reiser seg i mange av oss
qui se levant en nous se relèvent en nombre de nous

Some that arise in some of us arrive in each of us
noen som reiser seg i noen av oss kommer frem i hver av oss
qui se levant en nous se relèvent de chacun de nous

CAT IN THE THROAT

A lingual event is taking place, not in the voice but in the clearing of the throat.

Spitting out the most intimate and most irretrievable, the most naturalised source language, so-called mother tongue, is a dare, it is dangerous. It starts a whole process of re-embodying one's language's spaces.

The spittle can be resistant, unpleasant, potentially as well-aimed as a thrown shoe. Beckett's traffic from English to French is an expectoration of the English language's occupation on the colonised Irish body. His leitmotifs of speech loss, language stutter, assisted memory, gestural language all point to his fighting off one language with another language, transforming in the process both the spat-out source language and the adoptive language.

In French, to clear one's throat is to have a cat in the throat, avoir un chat dans la gorge. One needs to spit out a cat to clear one's throat. Literally, 'un crachat' is a spittle. One could also clear one's throat and realise that one has spat out French slang, une chatte, a pussy.

This adds and maintains a crucial libidinal and erotic bond with one's pussycat.

As I become aware that I'm trying to speak, my body morphs, my cat appears. Cat is the tone in my speech, its accentedness, its autography. Cat is my speech's subjective accent, the intonation of my verbal patterns, the stutter of my silencings, an all-round explicit accentedness. So what if I were to decide to speak with a cat in the throat?

English-speakers don't so much struggle with cats as with frogs. It's a croaking frog that one would need to spit out in English. Given the dubious and long-standing historical traffic of culinary jokes and insults between the French ('frogs') and the English ('rosbif') and bearing in mind the old wars of invasion and occupation between the two countries, one could here speculate that 'having a frog in the throat' resonates more with military and political history, and the known influence of French on the development of English vocabulary, than with strictly contemporary matters. Not so, if one believes John Ashbery's line: "I hear the toad crooning".

As many of us are finding ourselves with much increased frequency living in countries in which we were not born, or where we are first or second generation citizens, or long-standing residents, or new arrivants, there is an interrupted experience of the past and of the living locale, whether we do or don't experience ourselves as diasporic. Whoever needs to create an allegiance or a correspondence, sometimes seemingly from scratch, or from access-points hidden from view, to a mixed cultural background, to a complex living

jigsaw of multiple markers and untranslated biographical circum-
stances, will also often question what linguistic belonging means,
what fluency entails. To seek this out in the fullness of language, in
the connective and lubricated tissues of language, and around
language, is to speak and work with a cat in the throat.

So there is this friction inside the speaker's mouth. This friction on
the throat. Friction brings awareness of connection and of obstruc-
tion. The intake of breath, the raspy sound as one clears one's throat,
the spit that wells up, the sounds that follow, the words that form.

NOTES

MIDDLING ENGLISH

"Middling English" started out as "Short Aside on the Franker Tale" to address my growing interest in researching Middle English and Chaucerian structures. This early version was compiled by Nicky Marsh and Victoria Sheppard, after their *Pressure to Experiment* symposium at Southampton (with Joan Retallack, Jena Osman, Maggie O'Sullivan. Harriet Tarlo, Vincent Broqua et al) (*Jacket* #32, April 07). It was presented three years later, more or less in its current form as a keynote address at the Contemporary Women Writing Network (San Diego, July 10 2010). Many thanks to Clare Hanson, Edith Frampton and Anne Donady. An earthquake Richter scale 5.9 shook the ground during the talk and influenced the final reworking. Importantly, it is also the title I gave to my language-space-sound installation commissioned and co-produced by the John Hansard Gallery, Southampton (6 September-23 October 2010). The catalogue for the show features a specific version of this essay. For sources, see:

Charles Bernstein, "The Artifice of Absorption" in *A Poetics* (1992)

Andrea Brady, *Wildfire: A Verse Essay on Obscurity and Illumination* (2010)

Kamau Brathwaite, *ConVERSations with Nathaniel Mackey* (1999)

Hélène Cixous, *Three Steps on the Ladder of Writing* (1994)

Alessandro Portelli, *The Battle of Valle Giulia: Oral history and the Art of Dialogue* (1997)

Edouard Glissant, *Poetics of Relation*, tr. Betsy Wing (1990, 1997)

Russell Hoban, *Riddley Walker* (1980)

bpNichol, "22 Letter Alphabet", in *Imagining Language*, eds. S. McCaffery and J. Rasula (2001)

Monique Wittig, *The Lesbian Body*, tr. David Le Vay (1973, 1975)
Virginia Woolf, *Orlando* (1928)

SHORTER CHAUCER TALES

The language party of the "Shorter Chaucer Tales" was initially prompted and invited by Charles Bernstein and David Wallace to premiere at the New Chaucer Society's annual conference (New York, 28 July 2006). The first four pieces of the series, published here, were subsequently launched as four audiotexts and hosted on PennSound in October 2006, by Charles Bernstein, Al Filreis and Michael Hennessey. Thanks to all involved for their dedication, and especially to Charles Bernstein for prompting this crucial development in my work.

"The Host Tale" lists food and drink references in *The Canterbury Tales*. It first appeared in print in its current Middle English form in the Norwegian literary journal *Vagant* (Oslo, Spring 2007). Editors Audun Lindholm and Susanne Christensen let it pass for contemporary Norwegian preceded by a short preface.

"The Summer Tale" intersperses the online BBC news article "Polish ice cream ban for papal visit" (2006/05/25) with Chaucer quotes from the Summoner and Pardoner's Tales. Published in *Jacket* #31 (October 2006).

"The Franker Tale" includes: an excerpt from "Letter To Women For Beijing Conference" by Pope John Paul II, dated June 29 and released July 10, 1995 by the Vatican; Presence of Francis Bacon in his studio; *The Franklin Tale*; John Ashbery's *Variations, Calypso and Fugue*. Published in *Jacket* #32 (April 2007). As ever my gratitude to John Tranter and Pam Brown.

"The Not Tale" is a translation of a cross-section of Arcite's extravagant and moving funeral in "The Knight's Tale." It was first published in *Poetry* (July/August 2009) by guest-editor Kenneth Goldsmith.

"Fried Tale" was first published in *BOMB* #113 (Fall 2010) along with ink drawings from an earlier project, "21 Love Poems." With thanks to Monica de la Torre for featuring it in the magazine. Part 1 and 4 have been turned into broadsides, and feature also as audio recordings, read by Nicholas Rowe, in my installation *Middling English* at John Hansard gallery. They are reproduced in the show's catalogue.

Part 1. Spelling and some syntactical usage are taken from: Russell Hoban's *Riddley Walker*; Anthony Burgess's *Clockwork Orange*; *The Matrix*; British tabloid headlines; "Le Krach du Libéralisme" (*Manière de Voir*, #102, 2008). It quotes from: Derek Brewer's *Medieval Comic Tales* (1996) and "The Friar's Tale."

Part 2 is reconstructed from J.K. Galbraith's *Short history of Financial Euphoria* (1994). It quotes from *Riddley Walker* (1980) by Russell Hoban; "La Pompe à Phynances" blog by Frederic Lordon (26/03/2009); *The Guardian* newspaper.

Part 3 includes quotes from: the grime album *London Zoo* (2008) by The Bug; "C thru U" from alt hip hop *Fluorescent Black* (2009) by Anti Pop Consortium; "The Summoner's Tale".

Part 4 includes references to: "Maths cracks beer froth mystery" (BBC, 26/04/2007); pubs.com; opening lines of Derek Jarman's post-apocalyptic yet strangely intimate *Last of England* (1987), composed and directed at the height of the Thatcher years; the instating of Clause 28 criminalizing the "promotion of homosexuality," and the Falklands war.

TRANSCRIPTIONS

"Heaps" (from drawing), "Fuses" (from film) and "First Take, Track One (Roberta Flack can clean your soul – out)" (from song) celebrate ideas of dictation, transcription, chains of learning and interdependence. Transmission here is urgency and meticulous pleasure at material handling. Nancy Spero's *Codex Artaud* is never far from my mind. "Fuses (after Carolee Schneemann)" first appeared in *The Brooklyn*

Rail (NY, June 2005) with thanks to Monica de la Torre. It appeared in this "7th wave" version in *TEXT Festival Anthology*, ed. Tony Trehy (Bury Art Gallery, 2007). I have enjoyed the dialogue continued by Cheryl Donegan's *Refuses* (2009), a netplunder video work, which used "Fuses" as its initial structuring device.

GOAN ATOM

Goan Atom (1. Doll) was published by Krupskaya (San Francisco, 2001). It was spatialized by Jocelyn Saidenberg and the author. Early versions of the text appeared as "Les Jets de la Poupée" in Keith Tuma, ed. *The Oxford Anthology of Twentieth Century British and Irish Poetry* (1998) and in book form as *Jets-Poupée* (Rem Press, 1999). The final section was adapted for the page from an early installation piece, *Ambient Fish* (Hull Time-Based Arts, Root 1999).

Working references include: Hans Bellmer's nodal Poupée; Dolly the sheep; Alfred Jarry's *Ubu* plays; Unica Zürn's obsession with textual anagrams, her folded tied-up body as sculpted dehumanized mass; Cindy Sherman; Louise Bourgeois; Gertrude Stein's "Dolls should be seen"; *The Independent* newspaper; Bataille's Big Toe; queer and metamorphic anatomies. It is the first full-length piece in which I started exploring bilingual writing techniques, notably in the form of micro code-switches.

UNTITLED (homage Inger Christensen)

"Untitled (homage Inger Christensen)" was commissioned by the Danish magazine *Trappe Tusind* for a commemorative issue for the poet Inger Christensen. I did not finish the piece in time; it appears here more or less unchanged.

MATERIAL COMPOUNDS

"Material Compounds" started out as "Writing Time, Data Loss, Material Frictions." It was invited as a writer's talk for the University of Chicago and for Poets House, NY (2007). With thanks to Jen Scappetone and Stephen Motika.

CROPPER

Cropper exists in two versions ("2006" and "2008"). This is the unpublished "2010" version. Each version pursues with a slightly different emphasis the development of an autobiographic compositional structure. The Norwegian interjections connect up and intercept the main body of the piece, turning it into a bilingual syntax. In Norwegian, "som" is a conjunction that introduces relative sentences or sub-clauses. First commissioned by the online Norwegian magazine *NyPoesi* (#2, 2006) and its editor Paal Bjelke Andersen. This version was featured in the anthology *Infinite Difference: Other Poetries by UK Women Poets*, ed. Carrie Etter (Shearsman Books, 2010). Revised and designed with Marit Münzberg for release in a second version and limited edition by Torque Press (2008). During a research residency in Paris (April 2010) sponsored by the group Double Change and the research center IMAGER, I developed the third set of French propositional phrases. Many thanks to the editors and poets involved, to Marit for our collaborations, and to Piers Hugill and Peter Middleton for inviting the project to Torque.

CAT IN THE THROAT

"Cat in the Throat" was first published in *Jacket* #37 (early 2009). Subsequently translated into Swedish by Athena Farrokzhad for *Ord & Bild* (1:1:2009) and into Norwegian by Tone Halling for the bilingual exhibition catalogue *To be Heard is to be Seen* (Henie Onstad Museum, July-August 2009) curated by Tone Hansen. It featured in Katarina Dzjelar's bilingual exhibition catalogue *Parapoetics* (Tent Gallery, Rotterdam, Oct-Nov 2009), curated by Mariette Drölle. Published in BRAND #6 (Spring/Summer 2010), London. Warm thanks to the editors Cherry Smyth and Nina Rapi. It is published here in a very condensed version.

THANKS

This collection owes a lot to a great number of people. Many thanks are due to the editors, curators, publishers, writers, arts collaborators and friends named in the above notes, who have supported and facilitated my work.

In addition to which, I extend my gratitude to:

Nicky Marsh and Peter Middleton, University of Southampton, who helped me to secure the Arts and Humanities Research Council Fellowship that allowed me the time and focus to put together this collection. Marjorie Perloff for her support through the years.

Erin Moure for sharp editing and rapid response unit during the volume's various stages.

Kevin Mount for stepping in and providing great attentive design to this project. Christina McPhee for preparing the visual scans.

Romana Huk, Carol Watts, Vincent Broqua, Monica de la Torre, Martin Glaz Serup, Claire MacDonald, Rodney McMillian, Taylor Davis, Harriet Evans, my parents Aliette and Arvid Bergvall.

Friendship feeds art.

This book would not be what it is today without the commitment and dedication of Stephen Motika, my generous and indefatigable publisher, or without Molly McBerg, for constant and fine-tuned attention to the work's detail, and for all that moves.
Thank you doesn't cover it.

Caroline Bergvall is an international writer who works across media, languages and artforms. French-Norwegian, currently based in London. She grew up in Switzerland, Norway and France with longer periods in the US and England. Projects and research alternate between published writings pieces and performance-oriented, often sound-driven language projects. Her books *Goan Atom* (2001), *Éclat* (1996 & 2002), *Fig* (2005), are noted for their combination of performative, visual and literary textualities.

Her artistic and performance work has been commissioned and presented internationally. Most recent projects: Arnolfini Gallery, Bristol (w/ Ciarán Maher); John Hansard Gallery (Southampton); Hammer Museum, Los Angeles (w/ Rodney McMillian); The Poetry Marathon, Serpentine Gallery London; MoMA, New York; Tate Modern, London; Museum of Contemporary Arts, Antwerp. Her critical work pursues her interest in questions of new literacies, plurilingualism, body politics and accented practices.

She was the Director of the innovative and cross-arts writing program, Performance Writing, at Dartington College of Arts (1995-2000); Visiting Professor, Temple University (2005); Co-Chair MFA Writing, Bard College (2004-2007). Awarded an Arts and Humanities Research Council Fellowship in the Creative and Performing Arts, University of Southampton (2007-2010).

Nightboat Books, a nonprofit organization, seeks to develop audiences for writers whose work resists convention and transcends boundaries. We publish books rich with poignancy, intelligence, and risk. Please visit our website, **www.nightboat.org**, to learn about our titles and how you can support our future publications.

The following individuals have supported the publication of this book. We thank them for their generosity and commitment to the mission of Nightboat Books:

Kazim Ali
Sarah Heller
Elizabeth Motika
Marjorie Perloff
Benjamin Taylor

In addition, this book has been made possible, in part, by a grant from the New York State Council on the Arts Literature Program.

State of the Arts

NYSCA